HOME SENSE

W9-BBX-828

cowritten by
STEVE MILLER

contributing writers
MONICA CAJAYON
LEAH MATUSON

photography by
DOUG MYERS

 rayo *An Imprint of* HarperCollins *Publishers*

HOME SENSE

Simple Solutions to Enhance Where and How You Live

Eduardo Xol

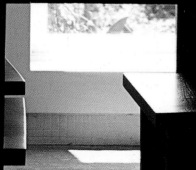

HOME SENSE. Copyright © 2007 by Eduardo Xol, Inc. All rights reserved. Printed in Mexico.
No part of this book may be used or reproduced in any manner whatsoever without written permission except in the
case of brief quotations embodied in critical articles and reviews. For information, address HarperCollins Publishers,
10 East 53rd Street, New York, NY 10022.

HarperCollins books may be purchased for educational, business, or sales promotional use. For information,
please write: Special Markets Department, HarperCollins Publishers, 10 East 53rd Street, New York, NY 10022.

FIRST EDITION

Book design by Janet M. Evans

The Library of Congress Cataloging-in-Publication Data

Xol, Eduardo.
    Home sense : simple solutions to enhance where and how you live / Eduardo Xol,
    cowritten by Steve Miller; contributions by Monica Cajayon, Leah Matuson;
    photography by Doug Myers.—1st ed.
        p.   cm.
            ISBN: 978-0-06-124976-1 (paperback)
            ISBN-10: 0-06-124976-9 (paperback)
        1. Interior decoration   I. Miller, Steve (Steve Alan), 1967-   II. Title.

    NK2115.X65   2007
    747—dc22

                                                                    2006049713

07 08 09 10 11   ID/RRD   10 9 8 7 6 5 4 3 2 1

I would like to dedicate this book to the memory of
Catalina Marquez and Maria de Jesus Carlin Marquez aka
"Tía Chuy," and to the four generations of living relatives
of the Marquez Family in Los Angeles ~

CONTENTS

INTRODUCTION

Over the course of this book, we will be looking at different rooms in many homes and examining how their owners dealt with issues such as lighting, storage, use of color, and the design challenges that present themselves in unusual spaces. One thing that I have noticed about the owners of each of these residences is that they are proud of their homes, no matter how small or large, and that they allowed their personalities to shine through in the design. Carmen Lopez used coral throughout her home as a theme, adding a beautiful palette from which to play off of. Jesse Acevedo went much more contemporary in his home overlooking Los Angeles, combining cement and glass with wonderful pieces of art and antiques, many from the Americas and Spain. The juxtaposition between old and new is one that translates well and allows for many days and nights of amazing conversation.

Home Sense is a small book with big ideas; ideas that you will be able to apply to your own home, room by room, no matter what your budget may be. You can create a sanctuary that you can be proud of and comfortable in. Some of the rooms in *Home Sense* might be a little daring for you as a whole. If this proves to be the case, focus on specific parts of the room that you like and make it your own. If a bright green bamboo commode with a brilliant red coral lamp is not for you, but you love the look and style, then come up with colors you would rather use and go from there. My hope is that your palette will expand and that you will look at your home a bit differently.

Here is your first assignment. Go to a room in your home that you would most like to change. Now, pick one item in that room, regardless of size, that you absolutely love and couldn't do without. I want you to use this as your main inspiration in your redesign. Whether it is a great accent pillow, a photograph, or your night stand, focus on it and write down five ways you think you can incorporate it into a fresh new look. You may want to paint the walls a similar or complimentary color or take furniture from other rooms in your home and incorporate those pieces into your vision. See, that wasn't so hard. Now you are a designer. Go forth and have fun. I can't wait to see what you come up with.

MY DESIGN PHILOSOPHY

When most people think of design, they usually think of the *visual* first. Next up are the concepts of *texture* and, hopefully, *composition*. It usually stops there. When most people think of a designer they think of an "expert" who will come into their homes and help them "make up their minds" and make their home look beautiful. The truth is that we are all designers of our own lives! Please excuse all of the "quotes," but so much of this seems "cliché."

Being a trained musician, I believe that composition is oftentimes more important than anything else. Like in music, if there isn't harmony then its opposite occurs: dissonance. Have you ever been next to someone who is singing along with the radio but can't match the notes at all? You want to plug your ears, right? Have you ever walked into a home or office where you clearly feel uncomfortable? These are situations where harmony is missing. Sometimes it is purposeful, whether it be musical or visual. In design, harmony is very important and can only exist when you think in terms of composition. All of the pieces need to work together and feel good. I repeat: *feel* good. As esoteric as it sounds, this is one of the most important concepts of design.

Because I started my design career as a landscape/exterior designer, I always love to bring the outdoors in and pull the inside out. I love creating outdoor rooms as well as adding as many natural and organic features to the interior of a home as I can. Ultimately though, I believe that the person who lives in the home must guide their own design process. You must trust your own "intuitive feng shui." I am a firm believer that we all have the capacity to design. Well, ok . . . let me take that back and be honest. Some of you ladies and gentlemen out there were never given that gene. But in the end, most of us have it. Some of us, however, tend to do better with guidance. I am hopeful that this book will guide you in a way that is simple and easy and gives you the confidence to ultimately design your own space.

How we live and what we do on a day-to-day basis has a huge affect on our lives, our health, and our happiness. Your home should be your *sanctuary*. Your bedroom is the temple of rejuvenation. Your bathroom can be your own personal spa. Your kitchen, dining room, and living room are the areas you should share with your friends and family to entertain and to build relationships. Many people do not understand how design comes into play here, but it does.

A few years ago, while I was developing my landscape design business, I took a side job teaching theater to inner-city kids in Los Angeles. Part of my training was learning the alternative teaching methods that taught me to use exercises on these kids that would stimulate all of their senses. I can't begin to tell you what a great effect this has had on my life and, ultimately, on my design philosophy.

At the end of my first season on *Extreme Makeover: Home Edition*, I was part of a project in which we had to makeover a new home for a man that had recently gone blind. The circumstances around how he lost his sight were tragic. When I met him, he was obviously in shock and very depressed. I took it upon myself to really do my best to change this man's quality of life. Besides having the good fortune to have had a blind design consultant on the show, I decided to do as much as I could with my eyes closed during that next week. I focused on the sounds I could create with water features, wind chimes, and plants; the textures I would use on the walls and the flooring; the candles and incense that might guide him in knowing exactly where he was; and lastly, visual color and texture for the rest of the family. Taste only came into play in coordination with smell in the kitchen, of course.

In the end, when he walked through the house, he had the biggest smile on his face. He later spoke of the independence his new home would give him in spite of his blindness. He began to *see* the world and his home in a new way. I would never design the same way again.

From that day forward, my design aesthetic and philosophy would be very clear. I would always design taking into consideration both the interior and the exterior of the environment I was working with. I would ultimately design to stimulate all of the senses of my client, and I would also do my best to "tune in" to my clients personal intuition.

Besides asking my clients what colors they preferred, I asked them what kind of music they listened to. I wanted to know what their favorite scents were and what foods they liked and disliked. This allowed me to come up with a very cohesive design for their homes. In the end, it wasn't about how much it cost, but rather how it was composed. It became about creating a complete environment that was harmonious and one that lent itself to a better quality of life for the people who lived in it. Designing for me became clear and simple. It made sense. HOME SENSE!

CHAPTER 1

Color

FOR MOST PEOPLE, COLOR IS ONE OF THE MOST IMPORTANT ELEMENTS OF DESIGN. COLOR CAN DEFINE ONE'S PERSONALITY AND AFFECT ONE'S MOOD.

We use color to express our feelings and to impact the environment in which we live. Specific colors are also said to have specific effects and responses. I do believe, however, that different cultures intepret color differently. I will give you a very specific example.

Recently, I was having a conversation with a dear friend and colleague about the color orange. He shared with me that in his design training during the eighties, he had been taught that the color orange was associated with a "bargain" or that which was "inexpensive," and therefore of lower quality.

Growing up in a Hispanic-American household during that same time, I learned that orange was a very common color and one that was culturally significant to me. It represented warmth and life and health! Recently, orange has become a very fashionable color as the influence of the retro culture of the '60s and '70s has come back into fashion. Coincidently, the influence of Hispanic culture in this country has also been of great influence lately, allowing the color orange to now have a positive and innovative effect in modern design in general. So, in the following color breakdown, let's start with orange.

ORANGE

Orange is a strong and vibrant color commonly associated with enthusiasm, strength, security, determination, attraction, success, encouragement, and stimulation. It isn't a color I would recommend to everybody, especially to those who still see it as a "bargain" color. If someone hasn't been accustomed to it, I would recommend using it as a color for an accent wall or for accessories. Even though it is one of my favorite colors, I wouldn't necessarily paint an entire room orange, but I would consider variations, like a pale tangerine, which is more palatable and could be integrated more easily.

RED

Red being the color of blood is associated with energy, strength, power, determination, passion, and love. It is an emotionally intense color that is considered to be aggressive. Red accessories in design are about bringing the concepts to the foreground.

I like to use red as an accent color in designs with Asian influences. I love red doors, pillows, and vases. Of course, the most common use of red in design is the red rose. There is nothing more beautiful than a bouquet of red roses to liven up a room and a special person's heart.

GREEN

The colors between green and blue are my absolute favorite. Green is the color of nature, symbolizing growth. The different shades of grass, leaves, trees, and plants inspire me and literally make me feel healthy. Color experts say that green has a great healing power and that it seems to be the gentlest color for the human eye. In design, the most obvious use of green is with the use of plants. This is also a great way to bring the outside in! I love to use different shades of green in almost all areas of design, although I would be cautious before painting an entire room green. I suggest testing several shades of green before making a commitment.

BLUE

Blue is the color of the ocean and the sky. It is considered to be beneficial to the mind and the body and is supposed to produce a tranquil and calming effect. In metaphysics and several native cultures, it is considered to be the most healing color.

When used in design, blue is a color that almost always works as it is attractive to both sexes, especially men. While blue is a common paint choice in a home, light blue is commonly used on walls, especially in bedrooms.

PURPLE

Purple obviously combines the power of blue and the energy of red and is considered a royal color. Although I find it to be a scarcely used color in design, I am seeing a strong trend with the use of lavender. I would also recommend using purple in a nursery or child's room.

YELLOW

The color of the sun is associated with joy and happiness. It is a color with lots of warmth and energy. Yet, when overused, yellow can have a negative effect.

I've noticed that yellow seems to be a color usually rejected by men. I happen to prefer it as another accent color and tend to lean toward the mustards. Again, like the red roses in a vase, sunflowers are my favorite natural yellow accessory, even if they are in a painting.

BROWN

Brown is the natural color of the Earth and a color commonly used in design through wood and leather. Men are definitely more likely to say that brown is one of their favorite colors. Over the last decade, dark brown has become a very popular color in contemporary design particularly in furniture and flooring. Recently, however, it seems that the use of lighter shades and/or varying shades of brown is becoming popular.

BLACK

Black is associated with elegance, formality, and mystery. Although black gives the feeling of perspective and depth and can make other colors stand out, it can easily make a space look and feel smaller than it is. Unless used with other bright colors for accessory, I usually avoid it as a primary choice with my interior design. It can be used to create more feelings of depth when used in accessories and small pieces of furniture.

WHITE

White is the color of perfection. It is clean and basic. One can never go wrong with white. I love the use of white on white bedding, flowing white curtains, and all white linen bathrooms. White on white, or white combined with creams or beige can be clean, elegant, and peaceful.

CHAPTER 2
The Bedroom

FOR MANY, THE BEDROOM IS A SANCTUARY. UNLIKE THE BATHROOM, WHICH IS SHARED WITH GUESTS, THE BEDROOM IS THE MOST PERSONAL OF SPACES WHERE ONE CAN RELAX WHEN THE DAY IS OVER AND FEEL COMPLETELY AT EASE, AWAY FROM PRYING EYES AND THE CHAOTIC OUTSIDE WORLD.

Since the bedroom is reserved for the most restorative and intimate of acts, and since we spend as much as one third of our lives in this space, many of us choose the colors, furnishings, and lighting of this room with extra care, keeping in mind that the details are meant to satisfy our own needs.

All bedrooms, whether large or small, have many functions. Though sleep is the primary one, in a large number of homes the bedroom has multiple personalities. Some house a small office while others share space with a living room or kitchen, as in the case of studio apartments. Still others include a space for entertaining guests with seating areas and places for conversation. Such nooks are also reflective of the owner's personality. Whatever the size, the intention is to create a space that allows you to relax. It might be enough to hang a curtain or shade that creates the illusion of a separate room. For others the effect is created through specially selected items laid out for display: pictures of loved ones, a favorite piece of art work or architectural find hung in a place of a headboard, a treasured piece of our childhood, or the stack of magazines and books that are always kept at arms reach.

Don't worry about what others do with their homes, or what's "in" or supposedly fashionable. Remember, you have to live with it, your friends don't. Whether you like contemporary or traditional, minimalism or a room full of keepsakes, be confident in your decisions and make it right for you. Maybe it is time to be a bit daring and use colors that you normally wouldn't, buy an area rug that makes you smile, splurge on 600 thread count sheets that you've been wanting because wrapping yourself in luxury is true bliss.

AN OPEN SPACE

An open floor plan and minimal amount of walls allows unfettered site lines from the bed, bathroom, and stairwell, making this room feel larger than it actually is. The soft white textured walls that surround a very low and architecturally designed platform bed compliment the white sheets. Beautifully designed thin stuffed pillows covered in a rough-hewed fabric from Japan along with the embroidered throw acts much like art as they do functional pieces.

The room is finished off by slate floors and an invitingly sexy conversation area which was fashioned by the placement of two low-slung custom club chairs and a large rectangular plush rug that serves to tie everything together.

THE FOCAL POINT

This guest bedroom provides the perfect opportunity for mixing antique furniture and photographs with modern elements. Niches were carved into the wall surrounding a gas burning fireplace to make up for the lack of storage areas. In this case, old candles and magazines add a subtle glow and sophistication to this room where no television is to be found. The eighteenth-century Spanish domed table, the focal point for which the room was designed around, makes an unconventional yet perfect side table, lengthening the wall against which it stands.

Remember, add pieces you love and cherish, even if they are not the most conventional of choice. The very fact that this bedside table doesn't fit the traditional definitions that we are used to, is what makes it all the more special. And in actuality, the hinged doors open up to reveal a large area in which necessary items can be stored neatly. So its purpose is aesthetic and practical.

A UNIFYING THEME

Beth Broderick Paetty's master bedroom was inspired by a book called *The Secret Life of Bees*, in which one of the characters lives in a room where every item is a shade of blue. Beth loves the color blue and finds it very peaceful. She was determined to find blue furnishings and draperies matching the deep blue paint on the walls.

The bed was formerly red velvet and has since been re-covered in a rich blue fabric with a diamond pattern. Adding the blue linens in various shades and patterns produced an elegant and unique look.

The chandeliers were found at a swap meet and gave the room a decidedly "movie star" look. Because the luxurious velvet curtains are unlined they quickly took on a faded character that adds warmth and a sense of timelessness to the room. Big blue chairs and an aqua dresser finished the space. The royal blue ottoman was also found at an estate sale. This room is a wonderful example of how to use a unifying theme, in this case color and period, to create a totally cohesive and committed look!

BRINGING THE INSIDE OUT

When Justus Grimalda first looked at this one bed-room condominium, he was taken by the expansive views of the city below. Unfortunately there was a wall that traveled the length of the entire apartment, there-by cutting off not only the bedroom from the rest of the condo but the brilliant views as well. The compart-mentalized feeling that this created was enough to deter him from buying. That changed, however, when he realized that the wall was not a structural require-ment. Soon after, he set about making a very open loft space while maintaining the integrity of a one bed-room home.

Adding a view from the bedroom was critical, since it would extend the site lines and make the home feel much larger than its 600 square feet. Still want-ing privacy for the bedroom, Justus installed an inno-vative wall of sliding opaque glass and metal doors, a look reminiscent of a shoji screen, though more con-temporary and resilient. Measuring 8.5 feet high by 18.5 feet long, this wall follows the same architectural lines as the prior structure, but adds a cleaner and much more youthful flare. The four connected panels slide back and forth effortlessly along a preset track in the ceiling and floor. Gutsy glass and stainless steel sliding doors were also installed along the balcony to maintain a consistent and cohesive feel, truly bringing the inside out and vice versa.

DESIGNING AROUND AN ARCHITECTURAL ELEMENT

The horizontal recessed window on the building's exterior front elevation is a defining architectural element that looks quite nice from the street. However, it made for a strange box over the master bed since the structure actually jutted into the bedroom itself. Instead of removing the window, a headboard element was designed around it. The headboard was originally built for an existing queen-size bed, leaving only an inch to spare on all sides. Once Phil Hammond decided to get a king-size bed, it became apparent that the opening was too small. Therefore a metal platform was purchased and a piece of foam was made to fill the space behind the king-size bed mattress, fitting into the wall surround. Sham pillows are used on top of the foam piece (which is wrapped in a white sheet). One of the benefits of the extra foam space (about 10 inches deep) is that the sham pillows can stay there when the bed is used. They don't have to be placed on the floor or on furniture like most sham pillow applications. Once the bed is made you cannot tell there is an extra piece to the bed. It gives the impression that the bed is larger than it is. The leather bench at the foot of the bed is a great addition, providing extra seating and a cool, clean, sophisticated look.

The shutters above the bed add a masculine look and also function to reduce light and noise from the outside. Floor-to-ceiling drapes next to the fireplace were added to soften and simplify the room since shutters on all the windows would have made the room quite fussy.

MIXING UP ROOMS

In the home of Gregory Han and Emily Ho, the first room you step into is the bedroom. An odd choice for most people, but in this very small city apartment, what they have chosen to do is original and creative

The room was originally designed to be the dining area. Early on, it was decided that it would be better used as the bedroom, so that they could use the main room as a living room in which to relax and entertain. This decision was solidified when their queen-size bed fit perfectly into the nook that once accommodated a built-in table and benches. A built-in china cabinet is now used to store personal items and display knick-knacks, sculpture, and books.

The bed is a case study handcrafted reproduction from the 1950s. Underneath, there is room to store a sizable collection of periodicals, out-of-season clothing, and miscellaneous items in long, sealable plastic containers.

Wall shelves were erected to display Gregory's toy collection. This was a way to group many small objects together, to bring color to the room, and to keep these items out of the cats' reach. The curtains were fashioned out of retro fabric found online.

Original artwork and prints, made by many of their friends, hang on the walls throughout the apartment. This is a great way to bring life and happiness to their small living space.

Because bedside tables wouldn't fit into the small nook along with the bed, corner shelves were installed instead, providing enough room for a lamp, flowers, books, and the like.

The initial concern about having given up a dining space has vanished. In fact, they find they don't even miss not having a formal dining room setting. Engaging friends and family in a more relaxed environment and taking their meals in their light-filled living room makes up for any slight inconveniences that might emerge.

BIGGER AND BRIGHTER

By gutting the ceiling and exposing the structural wood beams, Bodo Loerke's bedroom gained an extra foot in height. It can also be argued that because the beams are painted white, the room appears to be bigger and brighter and a bit more dramatic. The ceiling now serves as one of the main decorative design elements in the bedroom and stands out because of the dark brown textured walls and thick sea grass rug. Leather ottomans are used as side tables, a chic substitute for the common nightstand.

Instead of cluttering the ceiling with a bulky central fixture, small halogen lights on dimmers were installed at the four corners of the room. Since site lines are not interrupted, the long lines of the wood beams create a nice flow from one end of the room to the other.

The bed pulls together this small room w ith its dark frame that reminds one of thatched wood. It works well with the organic qualities of the other design features in the room. The white sheets with simple brown trim compliment the color scheme and connect well with the bed frame.

AN INSPIRING IMAGE

Kevin Morris's inspiration for this room was that of a ship where every square inch must be utilized efficiently. And in a room that is barely 10' x 10', space is a luxury not to be wasted. Slender bedside tables sit below long, narrowly built horizontal windows which are encased in aluminum frames making for a very light but modern look. These windows were placed as high as possible to make the room seem larger and to take advantage of the afternoon sun. Because a standard hanging closet was not an option, a wall of cabinets that are no more than 14" in depth were custom designed for the room, allowing for an abundant amount of space for linens, shoes, and folded clothing. Room for a flat panel television and stereo equipment were also added, making the room complete. A hallway closet was taken over for hanging clothes and other items.

The bedroom walls are covered in birch veneered plywood panels with a walnut stain, calming the room and softening the modern edges while still giving it warmth. Not wanting to clutter the room with unnecessary tabletop items, swing arm wall sconces in brushed steel were chosen for their architectural as well as functional appeal.

LIGHTING

This stunning four-poster bed is the focal point of Mary Randelman's bedroom and immediately sets the tone for the rest of the furnishings. The pink silk fabric adds a bit of fun to the bed's grand and elegant presence. The bed, which is backed in a soft cream-colored silk that compliments the light grey wallpaper, provides a cocoon-like environment that will no doubt make you spend many lazy hours reading in bed after a restful night's sleep. Well-appointed matching bed linens and pillows add to the overall comfort level.

Task lighting such as a lamp and chandelier would be practical additions in this room, while mood lighting using candles can add romance and allure to such a space. But if you want lighting that is easier to work with on a daily basis, wall sconces such as the ones floating above the pillows would be a great choice. Not only do they add a tremendous sense of style, but they also work very well with the historical aspects of this bed.

A PEACEFUL GUEST BEDROOM

Mary wanted her guest bedroom to be a sanctuary for friends when they visited her home. The eggplant colored walls provide a very intimate atmosphere and blends well with the upholstered furniture, curtains, and bed linens that were brought from her previous residence. The desk was specifically placed in the room for the use of laptops and portable equipment, but also functions as a stylish dressing table. It is both decorative and functional.

The highly carved gilded frames surrounding the antique mirror, along with the colorful paintings, make for a dramatic statement and supply additional texture to a room that is very comforting and inviting.

BEDROOM TIPS

Rearranging furniture that you already have will instantly refresh a room.

Buy new bedding and wrap yourself in high thread count linens for a great night's sleep.

Backing blinds and curtains with blackout material ensure darkness and long mornings in bed, but natural light is regenerative and healthy.

Swap out artwork that is currently hanging in your bedroom with another piece that is in your living room or dining room. A new look will instantly be created.

Lighting is just as important as your furniture and color scheme. The right accent lighting, floor, and wall fixtures will cut down on eye strain, reduce headaches, and allow you to create an atmosphere that is at once soothing and indicative of your personality. Interesting shapes and materials will add another dimension to your sanctuary.

Hide electronic equipment and wires in armoires and other cabinetry so as not to clutter up your room. While open and airy pieces might be nice, they tend to look messy and will make your room look a bit frantic.

CHAPTER 3

Storage and Display

HAVE YOU EVER HEARD SOMEONE COMPLAIN "WOW! I JUST HAVE TOO MUCH STORAGE! I DON'T KNOW WHAT I'M GOING TO DO!" NOT LIKELY. NO MATTER HOW MUCH STORAGE WE HAVE, WE NEVER SEEM TO HAVE ENOUGH.

SO HOW DO YOU MAKE THE MOST OF THE SPACE YOU HAVE? WELL, IT TAKES SOME PLANNING, SOME ORGANIZATION, SOME CREATIVITY, AND THE DIRE NEED FOR MORE SPACE TO HOUSE YOUR STUFF!

BOOKCASES

Take advantage of bookcases. Put all those books in one central area so that you can easily locate what you're looking for. Also, remember that bookcases are not just for books! Add a plant, favorite trinkets, photos, or your antique candlestick collection to the shelves. Not only will you tidy things up, but you'll also add interest to that area.

SHELVING

The use of shelving has long been a way to maximize space. Add shelves over and around the sink area, over a freestanding cabinet, credenza, or buffet. They can hold everything from small appliances, dishes, and glassware, to miscellaneous canisters. From wood to stainless steel to wire to beveled glass—you'll find shelves that are sure to fit your space and your style.

Shelf Units

If you have wall space, mount a shelf unit—either recessed or hung on the wall. Keep those often-used items within reach, show off those unique pottery jars that hold your shaving or makeup supplies and add a favorite accessory to the mix.

If you have space for only a single shelf, try using one made of beveled tempered glass and supported by decorative hardware. Add plants, favorite perfume bottles, mementos from vacations, or other treasured items for a decorative touch.

SHELF SHOWCASE

I am often asked how to make something as drab and boring as shelves into something stylish and fun. In this particular instance, these wooden shelves are not only functional, but also engaging to the eye. The thick dark boards are bold without being overpowering and deep enough to hold art as well as photographs. Another advantage is that they are not so large as to encumber the walkway. Unattractive or worn shelves take away from the pieces you display. Painting shelves a rich color or wrapping the shelves in fantastic fabric or colored leather will definitely create a whole new look, changing the environment and the feel of your room.

The eighteenth- and nineteenth-century deity carvings, which were chosen for their calming effect, set the tone for the rest of the design. This is a wall that would ordinarily not get a lot of attention. However, the patterned placement of the items coupled with the sculptural feel of the shelves themselves, now draw attention to this space.

Shelves should never be an afterthought on which to cram unwanted things. Design with the shelves in mind and use them to showcase family heirlooms, precious photos, and other fun collectibles.

TABLES AS CREATIVE STORAGE

Using end tables on either side of your couch provide you with more storage opportunities. A table that has drawers and a cabinet offers a great storage option for games, newspapers, and other shared items. Perhaps you can switch out that long table in the back of your couch for a long cabinet. You'll still have a stylish look, but with storage!

Dressing Up Your Table

The large abstract painting dominates this beautiful vignette and serves as the focal point of the design. It was important to add accessories that compliment the artwork without making the space look cluttered. In selecting these pieces, color was as important as height. The resulting combination nicely breaks up the horizontal look of the console. The pair of antique lanterns bring some uniformity and balance.

By layering a table in fabric that matches a bed, a dressing table fashioned from some old tables and drawers can become chic and elegant. Simple strips of Velcro hold everything together providing easy access to the drawers underneath. Adding a beautiful pair of lamps, bottles of perfume, personal photos, and an antique-framed mirror creates a luxurious setting to be enjoyed when getting ready to go out.

THE BATHROOM

Emily has a collection of vintage Avon containers, mostly in the shapes of ice cream and sweets that are humorously displayed using shadow boxes on the bathroom wall. This is a great way of aesthetically storing collections of smaller objects. To extend the sense of pop art and humor, even the roll of toilet paper gets its own shadow box.

This antique reproduction Asian themed wallpaper with bamboo motif was in this bathroom long before the chest of drawers and wall hanging showed up, but they go together beautifully. Matching wallpaper to your furniture or vice versa is definitely not an easy task. You need to think about the theme of your room, the personality you want it to have, and the atmosphere you want to create. In this case it is obvious that the bamboo is the unifying theme.

THE DINING ROOM

Where do you keep your good tablecloths? Your large serving pieces? All those things you use in the dining room? More often than not, many of those things end up being stored in the kitchen, which is not terribly convenient if you are setting the table for your guests. This is when a buffet, a china cabinet, a hutch, or a rolling cart come in handy.

Free up space in your kitchen by storing serving pieces along with table linens in your dining room buffet. Many buffets have several drawers along with cabinet areas and shelves for even more storage. Your china cabinet or hutch is also the perfect place to display your good china and crystal.

Use your serving cart as an additional serving area, as well as a portable bar area. With countless styles and finishes, many serving carts have drawers and cabinets for storing bar accessories, glasses, wines, and cordials. Another great thing is that serving carts are on wheels and, therefore, easy to move.

KITCHEN CABINETS, LAZY SUSANS, AND TILT-OUTS

Almost all kitchen cabinets come with shelves. So how can you make the most of the space inside your cabinets? For maximum efficiency, add pullout units to gain easy access to pots and pans, serving pieces, dishes, and glassware. Still other pullout units are made for stowing trash cans and recycling bins, to name just a few.

You might also choose from a variety of inside cabinet door-mounted wire racks for holding trash containers, spices, paper towels, plastic bags, and other kitchen utensils. Small, door-mounted storage trays are perfect for holding cleansers, soaps, and sponges as well as other kitchen items you might normally find under the sink or in the closet.

For that hard to reach space in the back of your cabinets, try using a lazy Susan to help you reach those pots and pans more easily.

If you don't have enough room for those wineglasses or even baking tins in your cabinets, make use of your space by installing unobtrusive stemware holders and grooves for your cookware.

Eliminate clutter around your kitchen sink with tilt-outs (also called tip-outs). A tilt-out is a small unit that fits in the false front of most kitchen sink cabinets and holds items such as sponges, soap, and dish wands.

THE CLOSET

Say goodbye to the bland and dysfunctional. This walk-in closet is transformed from an ugly duckling to a mod space with some very simple and inexpensive elements. Three colorful rugs were placed on top of the aging wood floors to form a seamless design from one end of the closet to the other, giving the effect that the room is longer. The rugs also provide comfort, since this closet also becomes a dressing area.

The shoe house serves two very distinct functions. The first is the more obvious, as it keeps your shoes in one place, and the closet free of clutter. Second, it creates another shelf for storage, which in a small closet is a great thing.

By including artwork and other personal touches, you can make your closet more distinctive. In the end you will take more pride in the way your closet looks and that will no doubt assist in making it more functional, organized, convenient, and pleasant to look at.

Before

Organizing Your Closet

Does your bedroom have a regular or a walk-in closet? Either way, with a myriad of closet kits and individual units available, you can now be the proud owner of a storage efficient closet! From swivel and pull-out pant suit and skirt racks, to pull-out baskets for sweaters, socks, tee shirts, and other personal items, there are now multiple ways to easily organize your closet. There are even shoe storage systems; tie, belt, and cap racks; cubes for clothing, purses, scarves, hats; and so much more. There are units that fit on the inside of the closet door, as well as multihook bars that fit over the top of the closet door. With all these options, you can finally have the closet that you've only dreamed of!

Decorating Your Closet Space

Using documentary wallpaper, which is a reproduction of historic wallpaper, Mary chose a French inspired wall covering that truly looks like a quilted tufted fabric giving a regal effect to the closet. Bright colors will make your closet a happier place to step into. The bust is a fun and innovative way to hold her jewelry, and makes a bold statement, giving people insight into her personality. The gold frame further brightens the room and matches the pulls on the drawers. Changing out the hardware on her furniture contributed to a whole new and refreshed look to her room.

STORAGE AND DISPLAY TIPS

Be creative. Think of storage and display as a design project to beautify your home, not just as an opportunity to make it more practical.

Storage and display furniture that are on wheels make it easier to change the composition of any room.

Don't forget that storage, display, and tabletop require specific lighting.

When displaying objects behind glass-fronted doors, be mindful of clutter. Keep the shelves clean and orderly for the best presentation.

CHAPTER 4

The Bathroom

TODAY THE BATHROOM HAS BECOME AS MUCH A STATEMENT OF THE OWNER'S PERSONALITY AS THEIR CAR OR CHOICE OF CLOTHING. IN BATHROOMS, SPACE SAVING FURNITURE, USE OF COLOR, NATURAL LIGHT, AND TEXTURES—SUCH AS STONE, TILE, AND FABRIC—MAKE A STRONG IMPACT. THOUGH SOME BATHROOMS

reflect the charming and careful details characteristic of the indulgent and design-conscious bather, the simplest of bathrooms can just as easily become a private haven of calm. And with a huge selection of products to choose from, it makes no difference if it's a one-bedroom apartment or a mansion with his and her suites, there are numerous ways of making even the smallest of bathrooms functional, serene, and inviting without maxing out the credit cards.

Some of my acquaintances have made their bathrooms as comfortable as any other room in their home. One placed her favorite chair and ottoman, along with a small side table that holds her design magazines, in her bathroom. Another, whose studio apartment has a bathroom big enough to fit only the essentials, splurged on a Japanese style soaking tub, sporting a showerhead fixture that makes Niagara Falls seem small when it's turned on. Now this was

a decadent personal choice. He also used wall fixtures and cabinetry in order to create more space for storage and give the room the appearance of being bigger than it actually is.

Many times, however, bathrooms require complete makeovers. This can be costly and overwhelming, so my advice is to take it one step at a time. Purchase furniture and design magazines and take the time to visit bed and bath stores. Choose a color you love and paint the walls first. After all, this creates the mood. Then decide on a sink and type of storage facility. Would a wall-mounted or cabinet-mounted sink be a better use of space? Would it increase your storage capacity? Or would a pedestal sink better fit with your design sensibilities. Step by step, you build your design scheme and soon enough your room will be finished.

MIRROR, MIRROR, ON THE WALL

Mirrors of all shapes and sizes adorn the walls of Beth Broderick Paetty's master bathroom. Now when she is getting ready to go out on the town, she knows what she looks like from all angles. From a design perspective, mirrors don't have to be of any particular size to give a room the illusion of added length and depth. Natural light is reflected from the window opposite the mirrors creating more light for a room that would normally have depended on artificial radiance. The overall effect is a sense of airiness.

PETITE BATHROOMS

This small powder room is no shrinking violet. There are several things you wouldn't expect from a 1950s bathroom left mostly in its original state. First, the faux fur fabric that is wrapped around a fluorescent light fixture is completely and utterly unexpected. On top of being a great design element it is a chic way of making a room over the top and fun. Second, the hanging chandelier now becomes a secondary light source, and its nontraditional placement, down and to the side of the sink is another focal point, totally negating the fact that the room is tiny. The chandelier also creates a wonderful silhouette in the mirror upon entering.

This little jewel box comes to life with a vibrant orange palette and wraparound mirrors. The space 2'7" x 7' is definitely small, but has a big personality. This redesign was completed with some paint, new hardware, and a new sink and countertop. The cabinet is the original, but was given a face-lift. The sleek white Carrara marble countertop is an elegant addition to this room as is the bespoke fixture in an effervescent orange. Keeping the space spare is important to the design. Clutter would have made the bathroom feel as small as it is and it would have erased that wow factor!

LESS CLUTTER, MORE LIGHT

The use of soothing green and brown porcelain tiles in the bathroom was inspired by the strong desire to bring nature indoors and to create a personal and tranquil environment. The joints of the wall tile were slightly staggered making for a more contemporary feel. Below the large mirror, the tile was rounded in order to give depth and length to the wall. Mirroring the entire wall takes advantage of the window that faces out toward the bedroom and balcony, allowing for a large amount of natural light to enter the room. This gives a beautiful expansive effect making the room appear bigger, and allows the owner to look out to the sky.

The storage unit, a stand-alone white lacquered cabinet that loosely draws upon the principles of the Japanese tansu, is a perfect way to keep a clean and minimal environment, while providing ample space for personal-care products, towels, and other bath and spa items. The fact that it doesn't sit flush on the floor creates a more visually appealing look while giving its owner the ability to place a thin scale out of the way.

By coordinating the shower curtain and window treatment with the color of the wall tiles and furnishings, a cohesive look was easily created. Ultimately this small space was given a well-deserved face-lift by taking advantage of highly reflective surfaces, natural light, and sleek furniture that minimizes clutter.

TRADITIONAL–CONTEMPORARY BALANCE

In his bathroom, as in the kitchen, Phil Drewry chose an Arabesque/Moorish design aesthetic. The small handmade tiles on the backsplash greatly compliment the larger soft hewed tiles on the counter, giving a great visual canvas. The lattice front cabinets keep the space from becoming too heavy. The traditional floors are partially covered by a Persian rug that gracefully spans the width of the room and connects the sink area to the shower. It also provides a nice splash of color in this room, which otherwise relies heavily on earth tones.

The built-in cabinets are framed in wood that matches the rest of the room, providing a unifying quality while the drawer pulls add a whimsical and carefree sensibility. With a nod to the contemporary, wall mounted fixtures and equally architectural sinks interact well with the surrounding elements, combining old world and contemporary living.

The spa-like shower room sports dual shower heads, floor-to-ceiling tile work and a bathtub that doubles as a bench when the steam is turned on. The clear glass partitions keep the space open and filled with light. This bathroom takes a nice transitional approach to design that is neither too contemporary, nor too traditional.

FUNCTIONAL, CLEAN, AND COMFORTABLE

The placement of the shower door is conveniently designed to open away from the sink, keeping the space functional, practical, and comfortable. The wall behind the mirror was designed to match the bed surround and is backlit to provide ample lighting at night. The one and only bathroom window used to be opaque glass which prevented the owner from seeing out and diffused the light that came in. Now the window is clear and is dressed with new shutters that provide privacy and allow for natural light to enter. A main design decision was the placement of one large sink instead of two little ones so there would be more counter space. The use of large, deep drawers instead of cabinets maximizes storage for personal accessories and toiletries that might normally go in a medicine chest and overflow onto the counter. The uncluttered and clean surfaces leave you with a sense of light and space.

THE LENGTHENING EFFECT

Being that this bathroom is only 6' x 8' and that it is the only bathroom in the house, it was very important to make this space inviting as well as practical. Ebony stained bamboo flooring was installed for its grounding and natural feel. A frosted glass window lets in natural light and provides privacy. The most impressive design element, however, is the floor-to-ceiling glass tiles that emphasize "high style" in this most minimal of spaces. A great trick is the very high placement of the shower rod, extending the site lines upward and making the room seem larger. The shower curtain hangs several inches below the rod on very thin chain links, which also exaggerates this lengthening effect.

With a multitude of storage options, a bar on chrome legs was chosen as much for its progressive attitude as for the four healthy-size drawers that it afforded. The organic shaped bowl that sits on top of the bar serves to differentiate the two pieces, giving each its due attention.

MINIMAL SERENITY

A modern Zen retreat with a contemporary twist is how Bodo Loerke's bathroom can be described. The walls are covered floor-to-ceiling with unfilled and honed travertine tiles, presenting a more rustic charm in a soft neutral color palette. Honing tiles strip away the shininess and present a matte or flat finish, which results in a less fussy look. Travertine is a resilient and attractive natural stone that can be used in many different areas of the home. The texture of the stone literally makes you want to run your fingers over it.

The floor is punctuated with hundreds of dark brown glass tiles that cohesively tie together the colors of the master bedroom, only feet away. The small squares are a nice juxtaposition to the large travertine tiles, creating visual boundaries that add to the overall design of the bathroom.

The cabinet is topped with a filled and honed travertine counter and gracefully shaped bowl. Its clean lines provide multiple storage spaces and ample room for towels and linens. The minimalist style provides an architectural highlight while still displaying a warm, serene look.

The Chinese wooden ladder is perfect for holding towels but also acts as a sculptural piece of art. Its great height gives the illusion of higher ceilings.

The chrome sconces above the cabinet are a nod to a more modern design and match the sink fixtures.

COMBINING TEXTURES
MAKE THE ROOM

Light and bright were the prerequisites given by Carmen Lopez when designing this guest bathroom. Floor-to-ceiling Carrera marble tiles and a console sink with a matching marble top allow for the natural light to bounce off these surfaces, filling the room with a dazzling and joyous feeling. The abundant use of the Carrera marble combined with the use of black-and-white lattice-patterned tile flooring creates a contemporary look with a bit of old world charm. When used in this manner it reminds one of a glorious five-star hotel.

An exquisite handmade shell mirror hangs serenely over luxuriously rich, silk, sea grass wallpaper that has been specifically treated for use in bathrooms.

In this bathroom, the combination of textures and materials dramatically softens the clean-lined surfaces of the marble and visually unifies the space as a complete design concept rather than acting as separate individual elements.

PAINT, TILES, KNOBS, AND HINGES

In this cabana bathroom little had to be done to make it into an exciting and vibrant space. You will notice the cabinet and countertop are large and spacious, allowing for great storage, normally not found in a smaller bathroom. Instead of ripping out and starting over, it was decided that new paint and flooring would do the trick nicely, and save the owners money for other parts of the house that needed more attention.

After stripping and sanding forty odd years of old paint and grime from the cabinet, several coats of high gloss red were applied in order to give the cabinet a deep, rich, textured look. Multiple coats of paint will increase the intensity of whatever it is you are painting. The red coloring definitely added a defining personality to this bathroom that makes it standout.

In addition to repainting, eighteen-inch charcoal-colored porcelain tiles were installed in place of six layers of old vinyl linoleum. The linoleum was cracking, old, and way past its expiration date. The combination of black and red worked very well for creating a sleek and fresh look. Also, the high gloss finish chosen for both paint and tile, reflect the natural light that comes in through a small window, creating a vibrant feel.

A CLEAN AND SIMPLE MAKEOVER

To go along with the contemporary nature of the home, this small bathroom, almost an afterthought for the original owners who hadn't updated it since 1963, was given an aesthetic face-lift on a very strict budget. A chunky sink and cabinet were replaced with an above-mounted sink and table, which highlights the deep basin and sculptural lines.

It would have been very easy to make this 4' x 5' room into a claustrophobic mess, but by keeping the design simple, clean, and minimalist, it was made into a little jewel box. The mirrors create a dual effect. The larger of the two mirrors reflects the whole bathroom making it appear larger, while the small swing-mounted mirror reflects the bouquet of native woods as well as the entry foyer to the house giving the room an abundance of natural light that was previously missing.

The honey-colored bamboo floors have a clean fresh look that compliments the cherry wood veneer of the sink's cabinetry. Adding two antique silk paintings in an aged ebony frame finishes the room in a nice combination of old and new. You will notice that the frames are a bit scuffed and imperfect. Sometimes placing pieces that are a bit off and rough around the edges can definitely soften a very contemporary room while adding to the homey feel of a more traditional setup.

AN AT-HOME SPA

After a long, hard day of work, a massage and a hot shower is pure bliss. Well, what's the next best thing? A bathroom that feels like one's own personal spa.

Creating a spa environment is easier than you may think. Elements such as soft music, trickling water, textured surfaces, and a scented bath are easy to create and go a long way in forming your own personal oasis. In this bathroom, several different devices were used to create harmonious ambiance, while still allowing for a large amount of storage space for toiletry items and audio equipment.

The dark-colored bamboo floors definitely soften this linear bathroom, while the floating glass splash wall continues the theme of openness and seamlessly integrates the shower with the rest of the room. The green translucent tiles in the sunken shower reflect the natural light that streams in from the floor-to-ceiling windows creating a shimmering glow.

ANTIQUE PIECES

With a nod to its 1930s European roots and utilitarian aesthetics, this bathroom is unfettered from spa-like indulgences and unnecessary features. Simple clean lines, gleaming chrome fixtures, and a floor-to-ceiling glass partition, which separates the tub and shower, add to a subtle and understated elegance. The marble surfaces and unadorned grey walls, so reminiscent of a billowy cloud, envelope you from all sides, creating a very quiet tone.

A focal point in the room is this sleek designed antique cabinet with clear glass doors. Because there is no closet in this bathroom, the cabinet has been carefully stocked with plush bath towels, luxurious bath products, fragrances, and other personal-care accessories. It is functional, practical, and stunning. Though it may take more time to keep things neat and orderly, the effect will payoff by creating a more beautiful room.

The antique chest of drawers with its built-up patina serves as a great host to a bold and sculptural sink that is unusually deep for a bathroom. Many times affordable furniture that you accidentally come upon at a flea market, yard sale, or a designer showroom, may in fact be the perfect piece that finishes off that trouble spot you have. Don't be afraid to use it for a purpose it wasn't intended for originally. Rather than being relegated to storage, this chest of drawers now beautifully functions as a countertop.

Flowers and shells are included to liven up the room and bring the outside in. The modern chrome mirror, light, and sink fixtures, cohesively work together to create a contemporary design in a traditional setting.

CLUTTER-FREE, OLD-WORLD CHARM

Functionality and practicality were as important as the look, since this room serves as the main bathroom in Don Winston's house. Wanting to keep the design of the bathroom reminiscent of its original early-twentieth-century construction, it was decided that simple clean lines would ultimately be best. The problem, however, lies in the fact that storage space is at a premium, making it very easy to start cluttering up the space with furniture and personal accessories.

First, a vintage claw-foot tub was installed, making this the main focus of the bathroom and a beautiful piece of art in its own right. Second, a new pedestal sink was installed that approximated the look of the tub. Because the pedestal sink takes up less room, it gives this bathroom a larger appearance. The tub was later refinished to give it a highly patinated look, which helped to brighten up the space. Innovative wall features were added to hold toiletry items and free up surface space. In addition, toothbrush and soap containers were hung on either side of a clear glass shelf, which holds large architectural glass jars. These details give a very contemporary and artistic character to the room. It is one that you wouldn't necessarily expect in this quintessential craftsman bathroom.

A PERSONAL OASIS

The objective in this master bathroom was to create a spa environment. This room now serves as a retreat from the noise and tension of the outside world. In this space, stress is replaced by a sense of calm and rejuvenation.

Because the area was narrow to begin with, a traditional bathtub was ruled out. Instead, a larger, hand crafted, and customized sunken shower was installed. The free-formed floating cement wall, so reminiscent of a piece of contemporary sculpture, was a perfect device to hide all the plumbing and keep within the design parameters that were originally laid out. A large opaque glass window stands behind the wall diffusing the natural light in a gauzy texture.

The architectural niche carved from one of the structurally required walls, has the same effect an exterior window would, allowing air, light, and a sense of space to flow in from the bedroom area.

The floating counters with mounted sinks were designed to look like the walls and seamlessly merge into their surroundings. This bathing room is a direct reflection of the owner's taste and his penchant for marrying contemporary design with rustic charm in elegant and unexpected ways.

A BREATHABLE SMALL SPACE

A small guest bathroom utilizes as much space as possible with built-in wall closets, hanging storage units, and very architectural bathroom appliances. Floor-to-ceiling, small, square-cut ceramic tiles line the bathroom, which gives the illusion of more height. The light color also helps to diminish the claustrophobic feeling produced in a small space. The clear glass on the doors allows light from the other room to enter as well as allowing the eye to travel from one end of the hallway to the other.

BATHROOM TIPS

Hang mirrors on the wall to make the room look bigger. Stylish bath accessories placed on a countertop will add a bit of glamour to your bathroom.

An infusion of color in a monochromatic setting is a fun way to let your personality shine.

Place your magazines, room spray, and extra rolls of toilet paper in a beautiful box or container and place it next to your toilet. It will not only add another unusual element to your bathroom, but it will also give you more storage space.

Don't be afraid of texture in your bathroom. Using black rock in your shower, golden bamboo on your floors, or even tissue paper motifs on your ceiling are great ways to give your bathroom a fantastic new look.

Install dimmers so that you have your choice of light intensity, whether you are in the shower, bath, shaving, or putting on makeup.

CHAPTER 5

Lighting

EVERYONE KNOWS THAT LIGHTING SIGNIFICANTLY INFLUENCES THE TONE OF A ROOM. PRACTICALLY SPEAKING, ONE CAN ADD EXTRA LIGHT TO A ROOM BY USING A DECORATIVE FLUSH OR SEMI-FLUSH CEILING FIXTURE. YOU CAN FIND A BROAD RANGE IN STYLES, FROM TRADITIONAL TO MODERN, EARLY AMERICAN TO SOUTHWESTERN, OLD-WORLD TO COUNTRY, ORGANIC DESIGNS TO URBAN CHIC, AND EVERYTHING ELSE IN BETWEEN. GIVEN THE COUNTLESS OPTIONS, IT IS BEST TO COORDINATE CEILING FIXTURES AND WALL FIXTURES FOR A PULLED TOGETHER LOOK. OTHERWISE, CHOOSE A STYLE THAT IS CONSISTENT WITH THE DOMINANT LOOK OF THE ROOM.

CEILING FIXTURES

Chandeliers, minichandeliers, or pendant type lighting work well over eating areas and create a more formal feeling. With so many shapes, sizes, colors, and finishes to choose from, you are sure to find one to your liking. To add to the ambiance of the room, place recessed lighting around the perimeter and the corners of the room.

Also remember to replace conventional light switches with dimmer switches. This gives you the option to create different moods and ensures that you get the right amount of light for your activity.

LIGHTING CHOICES

Choosing lighting shouldn't have to be overwhelming. Just think about your decor, your lifestyle, and your budget. Visit your local home or lighting store to get a hands-on feel for what might work best in your home.

When using a table lamp as your reading light source, be sure that the lamp's shade comes down low enough to hide the bulb from sight. If you can see the bulb, you will likely be getting some glare which can be annoying and also taxing on your eyes.

TABLE LAMPS

Fixtures and bases are important, but don't forget about the shades! Many table lamps used for reading have lamp shades that progressively become wider as you go from top to bottom. This makes for better light dispersion. Nevertheless, there are many options in style.

Decorating with lamp shades gives you the flexibility to create a mood, so why not change your lamp shades to reflect your own personal style. You can choose from empire to flare to box pleat, and more. There are also many colors, patterns, and materials to fit your decor and budget.

Good lighting for reading is a must, so it isn't enough to rely on your overhead light. An overhead light doesn't produce enough light on the page for your eyes to comfortably read for any length of time. So it is best to add a table lamp to your end tables or nightstands.

SWING ARM AND COURTEOUS LAMPS

Swing arm lamps are another option for lighting. These are generally placed on a wall above the bed, or above a sink.

When dealing with courteous lamps, if you're not the only one sleeping in your bed, and you'd like to use a wall-mounted fixture, purchase one that offers two light sources so that one can be turned off without affecting the other.

WALL SCONCES

Wall sconces can provide ambient lighting and decorative interest to a room. There are multiple ways to use them. For instance, try placing sconces on either side of a fireplace mantel, above a mantel, or along a hallway wall. Using sconces as wall decoration can produce a dramatic effect. Let your imagination be your guide. Keep in mind that many manufacturers make sconces that can be coordinated with other fixtures in the room for a pulled together look.

If you have very high walls, try mounting sconces higher as well. Play around with placement before mounting them to a wall. For down-lighting, use sconces with the opening on the bottom. For up-lighting, or to draw attention to beams or architectural details, choose from a large assortment of sconces with the opening on top.

LIGHTING TIPS

If room has a specific theme, it is always a nice idea to match your table lamps with your chandeliers.

Don't be afraid of color and texture when it comes to lighting.

Take into consideration the natural light from outside, whether it is day or night.

How low a chandelier hangs is an important part of your design aesthetic.

CHAPTER 6

The Kitchen

THE KITCHEN IS ONE OF MY FAVORITE ROOMS IN THE HOUSE. IT'S PROBABLY BECAUSE OF THE MEMORIES I HAVE OF MY GRANDMOTHER'S—MAMÁ CATITA— KITCHEN WHERE SHE, MY MOM, AND MY TÍAS COOKED THE MOST EXTRA- ORDINARY MEALS. THE SMELLS, THE LAUGHTER, THE CLANGING OF POTS AND PANS AS WELL AS MY SISTER, BROTHERS, AND COUSINS CARRYING ON, CREATED A UNIQUE SYMPHONY OF MUSIC, WHICH IS STILL VIVID TO ME TODAY.

Most of all, I remember the love that emanated from her "not too small, but not to big" kitchen, as she liked to say. In times of celebration and in times of sadness, Mamá Catita's kitchen became the place where family and friends gathered.

Decades later, the allure of the kitchen still holds true. The kitchen, more than any other room in the house, is where people congregate. It doesn't matter if you have a living room full of gadgets or a deck overlooking the twinkling lights of Los Angeles, kitch- ens have a special aura. For one thing, people know they are closer to the food and drink, satiating two very important needs. Second, kitchens are usually less formal. It is a place where people know they can relax and be less self-conscious. Kitchens are meant to get dirty, so a spill here or there is more tolerated than in a formal dining room or living room where the mood immediately changes when the wine gets knocked over onto the velvet sofa, or when the salsa hits the carpeting or splashes an unwanted punch of color on an heirloom rug.

The nice thing about the kitchen is that it is supposed to be utilitarian. The kitchen is where food is pre- pared, cooked, and oftentimes consumed. Whether you are in New York, Paris, Mexico City, or Barcelona, kitchens perform the same function and often look the same.

REMODELING A BOX

You wouldn't know it by looking at this kitchen now, but the original design was a box with walls on all sides and fluorescent lighting overhead. Not only was it claustrophobic, but it was also dark and not practical. The 1960s cabinetry and appliances would not work with the new minimalist aesthetic of the apartment. Also, since culinary activities are important to Justus, an open and airy space was needed to nourish the stomach as well as the soul.

Ultimately, the wall separating the kitchen from the living area was torn down, opening it up to natural light and producing a fantastic view while also creating an area conducive to entertaining. But in taking down the wall, storage and counter space was lost, which is problematic in a small kitchen. To make up for the lost space, a long peninsula was built that was deep enough to house large drawers for storage of pots, pans, and utensils, and wide enough so that the countertop could hold large amounts of food and beverages in the event of a party.

The countertops throughout the kitchen are made from Caeserstone. Its reflective honed surface makes the room look cleaner and definitely brighter. The dark stained wood drawers under the counters are a great balance to the obscured glass cabinets above the counter, which matches elements in the rest of the open loft space. By adding glass elements to cabinet doors, the kitchen is opened up. In the case of smaller spaces, this will give the perception of a larger area because the depth of site has increased.

THE STOVE

This fantastic O'Keefe & Merritt stove with its period hood and light fixture stand out in this very cool and comfortable 1950s era kitchen. The diamond pattern on the stainless steel backsplash really adds to the design statement.

MAXIMIZING SPACE IN A SMALL KITCHEN

The size and layout of the Ho-Han kitchen really proved to be the biggest challenge for designing and living in this small space. Because both Gregory and Emily enjoy cooking and baking, they were committed to redesigning a lay out that would allow for such activities.

To maximize space, additional wall shelves were installed above the stove. A hanging fruit basket, a wall rail, and a magnetic strip were also placed above the stove to hold additional food items and cooking utensils. An over-the-sink cutting board further helped create more counter space. One consequence of smaller confines was that they had to learn to make do with fewer, multipurpose dishes for cooking and serving.

A smaller outer room that shares space with the hot water heater and refrigerator also houses a vintage British kitchenette. This complements the design aesthetic of the kitchen. It has enough room to store dishes, small appliances, pots, pans, and more pantry items. It also has a drop-down leaf to create even more surface area.

A RUSTIC KITCHEN WITH CHARM

The rustic appearance of Phil Drewry's kitchen balances nicely with the modern and clean lines of many of the appliances and fixtures that he has installed. The open-faced lattice work door panels which cover many of the cabinets gives a warmth to the kitchen while adding an interesting design element into the mix. This lattice work design also allows for a lighter look, but still keeps the cabinet's contents hidden from view.

The overall kitchen design with its arched walls, soft-hewed, hand-crafted tiles, and many windows, complements the rest of the house and closely mirrors the master bathroom that utilizes much of the same elements.

The tile that covers the length of the wall and countertops gives great height and depth to the kitchen and adds to the old-world charm that the kitchen exudes. The peasant sink allows for easy cleanup from the countertop and can be utilized for many different projects. The small breakfast nook off the kitchen is entered through a gently arched doorway which contributes to the overall tranquil feeling. A built-in bench is also multifunctional due to the large amount of storage it provides. The paint color of the nook is the same as the kitchen, extending site lines and making the entire space feel bigger.

A MODERN TWIST

The original kitchen was closed off from the rest of the down-stairs area. Cabinets dominated the space, allowing for very little light and almost no flow to the rest of the house. It just wasn't a place where people would naturally gather, as in most kitchens. Keeping the footprint, the kitchen was completely redesigned to allow more light and was made more dynamic and exciting by tiling the walls in luminously painted glass tiles. The espresso-stained cabinets give a very rich and textured look.

A central design feature was a pass through space to the dining room from the kitchen. Instead of creating a small window-type opening, the wall behind two of the kitchen cabinets—from the ceiling to the countertop—was removed in order to create a vertical sculptural element and reinforce an impression of high ceilings in the kitchen.

By constructing a pass-through to the dining room and enlarging the entrance to the kitchen the owner has produced a feeling of openness that was certainly not original to the floor plan. This decision changes the aesthetic of the room and is reflective of the modernist tendency to erode the boundaries between spaces.

Removing some upper cabinets and replacing them with thick architecturally designed shelving allowed for the display of plates and glasses while leaving them easily accessible for use.

BACK TO THE ROOTS

The Kadel/Namias kitchen was faithfully restored to its late 1940s roots, but updated with modern conveniences for today's lifestyle. An avid baker, Rick Namias is a collector of cooking paraphernalia. He was adamant that the pots and pans, as well as his spices, be readily available when needed, but out of sight when not being used. His requirement during this remodel was to make the kitchen truly functional and to create a room in which guests could gather and relax with a glass of wine. The large picture window at the far end of the kitchen overlooks a tranquil backyard with walking paths, wild flowers, and fruit and nut bearing trees.

Honed absolute black granite was chosen for the countertops simply because he didn't want to deal with shiny surfaces that require a lot of attention and care. He actually looked forward to the stone building up a rich patina that would increase over time and give it a well-worn look.

The floors in this kitchen are a classic Armstrong tile in a diamond pattern. These are brand-new but evocative of the 1940s and 1950s. The diamond pattern makes the kitchen look much longer and wider than it actually is.

KEEPING THE ORIGINAL STYLE ALIVE

This small kitchen was gutted in order to create a room that was within keeping to the home's Spanish Deco architectural roots. Although Carmen doesn't cook as much as she used to, she entertains a lot, so it was important that the kitchen be warm and cozy but highly functional. Though the original footprint was kept, a second refrigerator and a double set of ovens were installed in the pantry hallway, right behind the wall of cabinets. This area functions as a small chef's kitchen. Now, when guests are over, the hired chefs can cook and not interfere with the flow of traffic.

The ebonized wood flooring is actually the original subfloor of the kitchen, which was refurbished and brought back to life. The distressed wood gives an aged European effect and another dose of measured refinement.

Floor-to-ceiling, off-white wall tiles with blue-and-white decorative trim are continued throughout the kitchen on the countertops and the backsplash, making it look like one continuous wall and giving the perception of a larger space. The tiles themselves were purposely inset with wider grout lines to give a more aged feel. Such choices helped to evoke the original style of the home.

The clear-glass mounted cabinets allow for Carmen's collections of colorful pottery to shine, while adding another color palette to this very soft and relaxed country-style kitchen. Her choice of cabinetry also provides easy access with no guesswork needed. The 1949 O'Keefe & Merritt vintage oven is placed next to a small counter with additional cabinetry offering another surface to be utilized. Completing the room is a chandelier that was a flea market purchase, adding something fun and different to the kitchen.

One of the things that I noticed most in this kitchen is that although the kitchen is newly built, everything looks like it belongs in a house of this age. I believe that this is very important in designing homes that have a strong sense of their period.

SMALL DETAILS MAKE A LARGE IMPRESSION

Kevin Morris's 6 x 12-foot kitchen doesn't have a lot of room in which to work, but what it lacks in space is made up for in a sleek modern design. Floating cabinets and storage units crafted in a highly polished cobalt blue, Carrera marble countertops and other reflective surfaces such as the modern glass tiles in shades of gray, blue, green, and cream, envelope the room and keep this galley space from becoming heavy and oppressive. A door with a large diffused glass center was installed at the far end of the kitchen, further extending the site lines. The washer/drier combination share the same depth as the counter and are kept hidden behind matching cabinet doors; a very functional use of a small space. Meanwhile, the refrigerator, stove, and hood are all fronted with stainless steel making for a cohesive and clean look throughout.

Capturing space wherever possible, the ceiling in the kitchen was taken up to the wood beams adding several feet, giving a loft-like feeling to this space. Modern track lights were installed across several beams, adding both direct and flood lighting without being intrusive. Finally, the doors to the kitchen, like every room in the house, were raised an extra six inches. So instead of the doors being 6'8", they are now 7'2", making an extraordinary difference when it comes to the illusion of size. Upon entering the front door, you can see the glass tile, marble countertops, and vibrant blue cabinets in one glance. Six inches might seem like nothing, but it is the small details that make such a large impression in a small space.

FOR THE AVID COOK AND ENTERTAINER

This is a kitchen with lots of space, but Mary has designed it to work in galley form. Since she loves to cook and regularly entertains, it was necessary that the appliances, utensils, and accessories be at arm's reach. In building and designing the island as her prep space, she accomplished her goals and gave herself twenty-four extra drawers for storage. The built-in cabinets with clear glass door fronts that surround the kitchen are used for her extensive collection of dishware, silver, and crystal, which she has accumulated over her lifetime. A separate food pantry was built just outside the kitchen where the washer and drier are housed. An extremely comfortable and relaxed breakfast nook which was designed to double as a bar area during a party lies in one corner of the kitchen. By utilizing the nook's table for bottles and glasses, the countertops are freed up for trays and other foods. A plush banquette is placed on one side of the table backed by walls of bookcases that house cookbooks from around the world and a flat screen television.

The all white painted kitchen is offset by the boldly colored vintage Documentary tiles in a yellow and brown motif. It is a jolt of color that is unexpected, but works well. Mary chose this design because it reminded her of her great-grandmother's home that meant so much to her.

A SANCTUARY IN A COTTAGE

Most cottages were small and simple structures used as retreat homes around popular vacation destinations. These homes offered minimal luxury. The atmosphere was comfortable and laid-back versus one of opulence. Today, cottages can be seen in the most urban of settings. When it comes to design, extraordinary creativity is taking place. The modern reinvention of the cottage consists of an open floor plan, which allows for an abundance of natural light. Gone are the small rooms with lots of walls and too few windows.

Christine Salmon wanted a place where she could simply relax and unwind after being away on business for weeks. For her, the kitchen is her sanctuary. She loves to cook and throw dinner parties. Therefore, it was important for the space to include ample countertop workspace, while preserving enough room for her guests. The open design of the kitchen allows multiple people to participate in the cooking process or simply hang out. A person walking from one room to another does not interrupt conversations in this setting. Another benefit is that everyone is still in one another's view in this kitchen.

The large number of storage cabinets and counter-tops allow for clutter-free surroundings and provide easy access to glassware and plates. The open front ebonized cabinet on the far left of the kitchen is a great use of stand-alone furniture. By keeping the piece door free, it allows the eye to continuously sweep from wall to wall without being interrupted, making the room seem larger.

The real focal point of the kitchen is the oversize stove-topped island which has elegant architectural lines reminiscent of a Spanish antique. Stained in deep rich ebony, it stands in contrast to the light colored counter-tops, but works so well paired with contemporary accents. The gas lines and other apparatus are concealed within one of the table legs, allowing for a seamless design scheme. This piece also adds additional counter space and entertainment areas for the dining room table, which is only a few feet away.

FUNCTIONAL YET TRADITIONAL

Wanting to keep a traditional feel for the kitchen, it was very important that this room be functional, using state-of-the-art appliances, without appearing to be so. The integrity of the structure was as important as the appliances that went into it. Wood floors were installed that closely matched the original flooring in the dining room, giving a more cohesive feel by connecting the kitchen to the rest of the house. The generously proportioned built-in cabinets are all new, but handcrafted to approximate the look they might have had in the early twentieth century. Everything from fine china to cookbooks can now be stored without creating a clutter.

Since the kitchen looks over a lushly landscaped backyard and entertainment area, the walls and the cabinets were painted white so as to not compete with the view. Keep in mind that by using white as the main room color and by installing white appliances, a small space will appear much larger and maneuverable than it actually is.

There will be an uninterrupted site line from one wall to the other. In any case, white is a wonderful color choice since it can work so well in traditional, contemporary, or mixed period environments without ever feeling dated.

With a nod to the contemporary a Silestone quartz countertop was added that is cool to the touch and virtually maintenance free. This countertop can definitely be considered the focal point of the kitchen. By opting not to install cabinets over the sink more counter space was made available allowing for two or more people to be in the kitchen while socializing and/or cooking. The beveled edges that are incorporated into the countertop is a more expensive option; however, details like this can make a beautiful kitchen standout and become lavish. The saying "it's all in the details," is very true.

KITCHEN TIPS

Ceramic tiles clean easily and not much maintenance is required.

Installing an under mount sink will eliminate dirt build-up and reduce bacteria that tends to get trapped in the crevices between countertop and sink.

Keep your kitchen organized in a way that you don't have to move very far to get what you need. The sink, oven, and refrigerators should be in reaching distance from one another. Unnecessary work is at a minimum, optimizing your time when preparing a feast for ten or an on-the-go meal for a busy lifestyle.

To make your kitchen appear cleaner, use earth tones, install stainless steel surfaces, and opt for dark-colored floors, whether wood, tile, or stone.

If you don't have windows that allow natural light to come in, use lighter wood veneers and finishes for your cabinetry.

For a cleaner look, mount your cabinetry to the ceiling with no space in between. Not only will it be more architectural, but your kitchen will also appear larger.

CHAPTER 7

The Home Office

THE COMPUTER AGE HAS HAD A HUGE INFLUENCE ON THE NEED FOR HOME OFFICES. MANY HOMES DON'T HAVE THE EXTRA SPACE FOR A DESK, LET ALONE A HOME OFFICE. MOST OF THE TIME IT IS THE KITCHEN TABLE THAT PULLS DOUBLE DUTY WHERE A LAPTOP AND FILE FOLDERS FIGHT FOR SPACE

with the tableware. But with ingenuity and some design creativity, home offices can be put together in many places that are not being utilized to their maximum space potential. You might even be able to seamlessly integrate your space into the overall design aesthetic of your residence. A chair that shares the same colors of your room is a good place to start. A desk with a glass surface will keep the space from getting too heavy if you want a lighter environment.

The most important thing to remember is to keep your space functional and practical. It won't do you any good to carve out some room that is not large enough for you to comfortably work. You can become anxious simply by looking at a piled work surface.

In most instances, you will be next to a wall of some sort, so utilize the space you have. Shelves and additional drawer space will provide you with additional work options. If you are facing a wall, paint it a different color than the rest of your space and hang some great pictures or inspirational sayings. It will give you a defining boundary and a place that you know is separate and distinct, even if there are no walls or doors separating you from the living space. Also, place items around you that are needed for your specific work task. You will get to the next "to do" on your list, but in the meantime, keep those files in a drawer or in your briefcase.

THE KITCHEN OFFICE

Beth spends a great deal of time in the kitchen, which doubles as her home office for several hours a day. The solution was to create a kitchen office that allows her to pursue several passions in the course of the day. The corner bookcase holds her vast and beloved collection of cookbooks and magazines, while the small TV allows her to keep up with the day's news when she is working or preparing dinner.

THE BEDROOM OFFICE

A functional working environment was created out of a very narrow space where a closet once was. By adding an attractive modern desk with room for all the necessary conveniences and a highly stylized and transparent Lucite chair, a look was devised that nicely integrates the small nook into the bedroom area. The resulting space is stylishly noticeable without being intrusive or overpowering.

THE CRAFTY OFFICE

The Ho-Han sewing room was originally a vanity closet that was converted into a sewing, study, and library area for Emily Ho. Although she does most of her sewing by hand, Emily keeps her grandmother's sewing machine on her desk along with a silhouette of her mom as a child. These items really personalize the space. As for her sewing supplies, she keeps them organized in yogurt jars, a vintage thread rack, a hatbox, and other fun boxes. Framed vintage patterns are hung on the wall, creating a nice decorative statement.

The original Bertoia chair was rescued from uncertain fate by Greg Han when living in San Francisco. On the shelves, paperbacks are organized in a tiered arrangement to accommodate more books.

With the curtains, made by Emily from her favorite vintage fabric, this room is colorful and fun without being over the top. It reflects Emily's personality and allows her to be as comfortable as possible in her little private area.

THE MULTIPURPOSE OFFICE

The office in the Ho-Han house was most likely utilized as a long sleeping porch that had been connected to the unit next door when the building was first constructed. It is now, however, used as an office, sunroom, and reading room. And most important, it is the cats' favorite room.

Sunburst designed curtain panels cover the wall of windows and are heavy enough to block the glare when working on the computer, but transparent enough to allow sufficient lighting for reading and growing terrarium plants.

The long wood bench below the windows serves as both a seat and storage unit. The orange colored cushion, which was made by Emily from outdoor fabric, picks up some of the orange from the living room. This detail helps to cohesively bring everything together.

AN ANTIQUE WRITING SECRETARY

This highly decorative French eighteenth-century-style writing secretary with chinoiserie and floral decorations is the perfect place to compose those long handwritten letters to friends and family. Beautiful papers and bound leather diaries fit neatly into the multiple shelves, while antique writing utensils and an inkwell finish off a stunning visual presence in one corner of the bedroom.

HOME OFFICE TIPS

Close the door or put up a screen to separate you from the rest of your home. Make your time as productive as possible.

Choose a chair that fits your body type. There is nothing worse than an aching back or a sore neck.

Place your home office near a window so you can see the outside and have some natural light enter your space. It will mentally stimulate you and allow you to work longer than if you had only task lighting as your primary source.

Make sure you have a large enough space to place your essential items. And keep this area clean and well organized. A cluttered desk will make you edgy and less productive.

If your working space proves too small, add shelves and additional storage to give yourself command of your domain.

Create a daily to-do list so you won't procrastinate. A few minutes here and there will add up very quickly. Get your work done and then enjoy yourself.

CHAPTER 8

The Dining Room

WHY IS IT THAT THE DINING ROOM SEEMS TO BE THE LEAST USED ROOM IN THE HOME THESE DAYS? MOST PEOPLE I KNOW WHO HAVE A DINING ROOM RARELY USE IT EXCEPT WHEN THE IN-LAWS ARE OVER OR WHEN A FAMILY MEETING HAS BEEN CALLED. AND WHEN A FAMILY TALK REQUIRES SUCH FORMALITY, EVERYONE KNOWS SOMETHING HEAVY IS ABOUT TO BE DISCUSSED. HOWEVER,

growing up in my family, it was just the opposite. People sat at the dining table and ate together, on a regular basis, though I will admit that the china and good linens were reserved for special guests and/or special occasions. And as for the wedding silverware, it almost never came out, since we all dreaded having to polish it. In any case, fine tableware or not, at 6:30 P.M. I could always count on sharing a fantastic meal with my family.

How times do change. Today, the kitchen is where most families eat their daily meals. Even very young kids know not to play in the dining room where fragile family keepsakes, crystal stemware, and other prized delicate objects are kept. The dining room has been put on a pedestal for far too long. I say we change that tradition starting today. Open up your dining room to friends and family. Paint it a bright color. Place comfortable furniture in this room, like high back chairs that allow you to savor long meals and delicious desserts while enjoying good company into the late hours of the night. And as far as I am concerned, this is a room where family photos should be hung, rather than objects awarded museum-like status. Similarly, collections and other objects of curiosity should be displayed with pride and made available for guests to handle freely. My rule is, if you're afraid that the kids will break it, take it out of the dining room.

SPENDING MORE TIME IN YOUR DINING ROOM

Over the years, friends have told me of memorable meals enjoyed in the dining room when the extended family has gotten together. In most cases, everyone has described the warm and infectious laughter that has permeated the room, characteristic of holiday reminiscing. Whether it's Thanksgiving or Passover, Christmas or the late night meals of Ramadan, the dining room is most definitely a repository of memories. But sadly, it is a room that for some reason has become off-limits most of the year. A way to make it less formal is to open up the walls and allow the space to flow into the kitchen where most people congregate. In this way, more light will get in, thus creating a more congenial place to relax. After all, a less restrictive space calls for a less restrictive tone.

This marriage of space also allows the guests to enjoy the smells emanating from the kitchen stove tops and oven and creates a down-to-earth approach to entertaining. But, if a knock down is not in your future, then as I wrote earlier, soften the dining room with lighter and brighter furniture and colors. Opt for sheer curtains instead of heavier fabrics, choose less ornate furniture in favor of a more linear look. It doesn't mean you have to completely forsake your traditional or eclectic style for the stark bareness of new modernism. But it does mean that you will consciously pick pieces that will make you and your guests more willing to spend time in the dining room. There *is* such a thing as mixing comfort with high style!

A WELCOMING ROOM

This charming dining room is enclosed on three sides by long windows that look out to a beautiful patio, which houses a potting garden. The large refectory table holds old-growth geraniums and other flowers that have been cultivated over a long period of time. The look is at once alluring and romantic, and even a little nostalgic. Family and friends like to take their meals in this room because of its inviting qualities. The simple furniture is both comfortable and charming while the table is an inviting centerpiece to this small room.

The collection of Mexican pottery and other antiques from the Americas gives the table a very special and ethnic feel, livening up this dining area.

This dining room, full of natural light, flows seamlessly from the kitchen to the living room, truly allowing for intimate dinners for two or a fiesta for ten!

ELEGANT AND INVITING

In this home, breakfast is served in understated elegance, reminiscent of a French pied-à-terre. The gracious design brings with it a timeless sense of old-world grandeur. Rich in color and texture, this room is the perfect complement to the eclectic character of the rest of the house. Asian objects share the spotlight with furniture bought at flea markets in New York and art work purchased from galleries in Europe.

The round table for two with center flaring legs is a perfect addition to a room that is about 7' x 7'. The two slip-covered chairs in off-white linen with monogrammed backs add a certain regal quality to the space. The shutters, painted in pure white, control the amount of light in this naturally dark space, instantly creating mood and atmosphere. The valance and matching curtains provide the finishing touches to the room, the vertical stripes giving the room a sense of height.

The breakfast nook is just off a very small entrance foyer. By placing the chandelier in the site line as soon as you walk in, it gives the impression that the room is part of the foyer, instantly increasing the size of the surroundings and making for a more welcoming environment.

THE FORMAL DINING TABLE

Beth Broderick Paetty's dining room was a big challenge for her. She wanted a formal table that would seat ten, but finding 1950s period pieces for a dining room proved to be difficult. She was looking for something more elegant than what most people would consider to be typical 50s.

She finally found a huge table that sits on two giant urns, which form the base. The gold edging ties the wooden surface to its foundation. What made this table perfect for her home was the fact that the eight chairs it came with were all caned backed and upholstered in white leather. Though it took a bit of time to find, the table was exactly what she envisioned.

NATURAL LIGHT AND
A SENSE OF OPENNESS

In Luigi Irauzqui's house, the dining room embodies the home's Spanish Colonial roots. Generously size antiqued slate floors, large archways, and a warm color palette on highly textured walls gives one the feeling of being in the Spanish countryside.

The kitchen, in its present location, now flows into the dining room which is only a step away from the living room. This makes it easy to entertain guests and shepherd them from one room to the next. The archways and clear-glass-paneled doors gives this compact dining area a sense of scale and openness.

The French doors on one side of the dining room leads to a vine covered courtyard with a large central fountain, making this environment perfect for indoor/outdoor living. The natural light that embraces the dining room also lights part of the living room, creating a different ambiance depending on the time of day. Being aware of how the light affects the colors on your wall to the flowers on your table is important to keep in mind when designing.

LIVING/DINING AREA

The living room and dining room occupy most of Phil's downstairs living space. The living room is sectioned off into a very contemporary and inviting space with stylish furnishings and a large rug that unifies all of the pieces. The dining area is all about the table and how it is dressed. It feels separate and distinct because it has its own personality, but is still part of the whole room. A great flow is created whereby guests can transition from the living room to the dining table easily. Flow is a very important element in design. The placement of the table near the kitchen pass through allows for easy serving and entertaining. Nobody has to walk far to accomplish what they want.

One large window shade was used over three windows in the dining room in order to create a single element. Turning three windows into one large element keeps the small space from feeling busy and cluttered.

KITCHEN AND DINING COMBINED

The open floor plan combining the kitchen and dining room underscored Christine Salmon's commitment to practical and efficient living. The combined rooms allow for easy entertaining, while the continuity in color makes the space appear larger. Careful furniture placement is what distinguishes the two rooms.

This simple and low-key dining room reflects the easy going and comfortable qualities that Christine wanted in her home. A more relaxed lifestyle is expressed by choosing to upholster her dining room chairs in light colors and fabrics.

The small crystal chandelier that hangs over the table adds a bit of whimsical design that is unexpected and welcome in this unfussy dining room. Lighting makes a strong statement as well. By putting the chandelier on a dimmer switch, you can create an entirely different atmosphere for your evening soirees.

FORMAL AND FUN

This is a formal dining room with influences grounded in European and Asian furnishings. However, the rule in Carmen's house is that everyone is to have fun. Red wine or white, colas or clear sodas, sauces or spices, it doesn't matter. Her house is meant to bring people together and for people to enjoy themselves in a casual environment.

The large oval table with gracefully carved legs encourages conversation and fosters friendships among all guests, unlike square or rectangular tables which tend to isolate people from those at the other end. Anchoring the room are the various pieces of furniture and accessories that Carmen has bought during her travels. She buys what she likes and not what she feels will fit best. By doing so, the room will stay fresh for many years to come. You're not apt to get bored as you would if you bought everything at a local home store where things are massed produced by the thousands and where your friends and their friends have the same thing. There is by no means nothing wrong with that, but why not buy objects that bring back a great memory and make you smile for years to come.

Very few people I know buy entire rooms of completely matching furniture. It is more fun to mix it up a bit, throwing in an unexpected color here or a funky chandelier there. Two large arched windows are accentuated with hand-painted curtains from India and are hung right below the crown molding, giving the illusion of a higher ceiling and increasing the grand style of the room.

The proud Chinese chest of drawers is approximately 100 years old. An elegant collection of blue and white vases grouped in various sizes offers additional height and a certain gravity to the overall look. The vases are surrounded on either side by two aesthetically pruned plants in matching pots. A large oil painting of a dog and a pair of sconces decorated with stalks of wheat blowing in the wind add to the eclectic and elegant room. The two armchairs on either side of the chest are painted in the same rich black, popping in front of the light and airy painted walls. The striped fabric cushions further provide a nice dash of color.

On the opposite wall, a Victorian hutch shows off Carmen's collection of antique porcelain and silverware. Surrounding the hutch are antique etchings and a pair of lanterns that may seem out of place, but add greatly to the character and personality of this room. The room is brought together by the large sea grass rug that leaves enough room for the wonderful patina of the wood floors to peak through.

THREE TABLES ROLLED INTO ONE

Kevin Morris's house is designed around his lifestyle. Knowing that he likes to have friends and family over, a dining table was important to consider in the overall scheme. The problem is that there wasn't enough space for an actual dining room. What evolved was a multifunctional table which serves as a dining table, a display table, and a work station.

As a dining table it is convenient to the kitchen because it receives an abundance of natural light from the floor-to-ceiling window behind it and offers an unobstructed view to the television. The table can also be used as a bar area and a place where hors d'oeuvres are placed, freeing up the counter space in the kitchen for other needs. The well-proportioned, yet neatly tailored chairs with nail head appliqués, add a sense of height to the table, which makes for a very inviting place.

The use of the table as a display option was important to Kevin in order to show his treasured objects d'art that he has collected during his travels. The pieces accentuate the glass tabletop and chrome base, creating a softer environment. The large Buddha head almost becomes the focal point of the room, serving as an immediate conversation piece.

Eduardo Xol

A CLASSIC

The open living/dining room creates a unifying design plan that not only brings the two rooms seamlessly together, but also allows each room to stand on its own. In other words, each room has its own timeless design. The classic look that was chosen, both elegant and refined, did just that.

The muted colors of the room are offset by the original thick-planked wainscoting, which was painted a flat white to give more light to the room. In this case, the wainscoting also conveys more intimate proportions and warmth, which is sometimes hard to accomplish with open floor plans.

In keeping with the classic appearance, the table is set with a collection of silver candlesticks, antique glassware and china, as well as fine linens. The traditional place settings suggest a subtle look that is absolutely evocative of understated elegance and style. Adding a generous grouping of votive candles to the table allows the host to turn down the lights, creating a soothing environment for tranquil entertaining. The floral arrangement of white Star Gazers provides an additional element of light while bathing the room in fragrance. Note that while it is a full bouquet, it still allows the guests to see one another, without interrupting conversation.

LESS IS ALWAYS MORE

This small, but charming dining room in white is a great example of how the wall accents can give a room a very special quality.

When room is tight, don't cram. It won't make the room look finished or complete. Less is always more when the room is tastefully furnished and accessorized. Showing the legs of chairs and tables will also give the room a larger feel than if you slipcover your furniture or put a tablecloth on the table.

The various mirrors and other ethnic objects on the main wall create an effect that makes the room appear larger. The mirrors reflect the sunlight coming in from the windows, giving the room a brighter disposition. Sunlight always makes a room more appealing, turning lazy breakfasts into hearty lunches and fostering great conversation all the while.

Keeping the table set informally is a nice way to dress a table when it is not being used. It gives the room a lived-in feeling and adds color and warmth to the room.

DINING ROOM TIPS

Yellows and oranges are most associated with food and stimulate brain activity.

A glossy finish on your ceiling will enhance the light reflecting from your lighting fixtures and candles.

Paint the inside of your window sills a light color so the sun will reflect more light. The room will instantly become friendlier and more conducive to entertaining.

The dining room is a great place to show off your collectibles and the fruit of your hobbies.

Allow the outside to come in. Bring some of your potted plants inside during dinner parties or arrange several great bouquets of your favorite flowers.

In space challenged dining rooms, choose furniture with exposed legs and glass, and mirrored surfaces to give the illusion of roominess. Stay away from skirted fabric that hangs down to the floor.

CHAPTER 9

Design for Entertaining

ENTERTAINING IS A VERY IMPORTANT ELEMENT TO TAKE INTO CONSIDERATION WHEN DESIGNING YOUR HOME. IN MY CULTURE, AS IN MANY, ENTERTAINMENT—ESPECIALLY IN TERMS OF FAMILY GATHERINGS—HAS HAD A GREAT INFLUENCE ON THE DESIGN DECISIONS MY FAMILY AND I HAVE MADE THROUGHOUT THE YEARS.

The most important element to identify, when considering entertaining in the context of design, is one's own lifestyle. Who are you, in a social setting? Are you a natural host? Do you like to cook your own dinners? Will you be entertaining guests with children? So many people never think about these questions when they are designing their homes. They encounter the challenges after the fact.

To open up your home to others is such a gift. The design of your home is an extension of who you are. People who walk into your apartment, house, or garden experience a piece of you. I can't tell you how many times I have walked into someone's space and realized that they don't understand this concept. First and foremost, your home is *for you*. It should be comfortable and practical and work for the needs of your lifestyle. Next, it is an extension of who you are. Your guests and friends are usually living expressions of your life, so ask yourself the question: Who does your home invite? How do your guests feel? Who do you aspire to be? These are important questions that should be taken into consideration when designing a space for entertaining.

For me, tradition takes an important role in defining your entertaining space. Friendly dinners and family gatherings will demand a beautiful and functional environment like that in the home of Don Winston or Scott and Beth.

For other people, simpler entertaining is the choice. Thus cocktail party settings are preferred. We can see different examples of bar setups conducive to great cocktail party scenarios.

Whether it's a full sit down dinner or a cocktail party, the ability to entertain in your home should always be taken into consideration in your design.

A CLASSIC BAR AT HOME

In Luigi Irauzqui's house we have a beautifully functional full bar, complete with storage and service areas set in the wall of his den. Although he has all of the products and materials he needs, you can see that everything is placed with thought, giving this bar a certain charm.

The cabinets and hardware combined with the tile backsplash give this bar an elegant gentleman's feel while still working with the Spanish Colonial style of his home. As for the service sink and wine storage, both are functional and stylish. And the accessories he uses are all of the highest quality.

He enjoys treating his clients with first-rate hospitality offering them their choice of beverage served in Waterford crystal.

THE COCKTAIL SETUP

Some people prefer not to display their bar at all times. Keeping a bar in a cabinet is a great idea. Hanging glasses from a rack above the spirits and necessary accessories provides your guests with everything they need. When company is over or the party is taking place, the bar-cabinet is open and can allow the bar to be a self-serve situation. When the party is over and the bar is closed, so is the cabinet with it's contents hidden.

In Beth Broderick Paetty's house, we have the beautiful retro bar that actually takes aesthetics into consideration before function. This French 1950s bar speaks of late nights and dashing men and women shaking martinis and bopping to jazz. The gold cage and burnished walnut finish has a timeless feel and holds its own in any surrounding. Many of the pieces she has are, in fact, art pieces. She sometimes switches some of the glasses out when entertaining for larger groups, but confesses that she loves to serve her close friends in the period glassware she cherishes so much!

A movable cart is a practical way to be able to have your bar wherever you need it. As people move from one room to another, so can the location of the bar. Don prefers this stainless steel frame with three levels. He keeps his most commonly used spirits on the top shelf, glassware on the second, and mixers and less commonly used spirits on the bottom.

BAR TIPS

Stock your bar with at least half a dozen glasses for your basic drinks:

- 6 Martini
- 6 Rocks glasses
- 6 Highball
- 6 Wine
- 6 Beer mugs

Start off with your basic accessories:

- Ice bucket
- Shaker
- Pitcher

If you are going to keep your bar out in the open, buy attractive bottles and decanters that look good in your room.

Your bar should match the rest of the room. Keep the design and motif the same.

Modify your bar according to the guests you will be entertaining.

Consider investing in quality barware since it will serve a dual purpose: design and function.

CHAPTER 10

The Living Room

THE LIVING ROOM REMINDS ME OF FAMILY TIME; MOMENTS THAT YOU CHERISH WHEN LOOKED BACK ON. GROWING UP, WE WOULD ALL MOVE FROM THE KITCHEN TABLE TO THE LIVING ROOM WHERE MY DAD WOULD TELL US SOME GREAT STORIES ABOUT HIS CHILDHOOD AND THE COLORFUL LIFE HE LED ON

a ranch in a small town in Mexico. Without question, my parents' aesthetic was definitely unique and indicative of a cross-cultural lifestyle and mindset. Though our 19-inch black-and-white manual-control TV often droned on in the background, our attention was focused on Dad.

Like my grandma Catita's kitchen, our living room was a happy place. I will say, however, that the furniture was more durable than comfortable. Our couch consisted of large pillows on a rustic wooden Mexican bench, the top of which was carved with a simple swirling design. We also had a matching side chair, a very unusual octagonal-shaped center table, leather-weaved bar stools that rested against a small bar, and matching leather sitting chairs that surrounded the game table, which most guests vied for. To offset all the woodwork, my parents had mirrored panels installed onto one entire wall. Think 1970s suburbia meets Hacienda chic. The decor was simple, most definitely ethnic, and a bit artsy, too: My father's oil paintings of gardens and plazas in Mexico and his self-portraits decorated the walls of our home.

As I grew up, times changed, as did the furniture. My parents eventually opted for softer lines and a more traditional composition. But the one thing that has not changed is the vibe that I felt as a child, the feeling of always being welcome. I hope your home also evokes such fond memories. I hope board games are played, television is watched, and conversations are had in the rooms that are supposed to be most "lived" in.

The living rooms that are showcased in this book all have at least two things in common. First, these rooms show the personalities of their owners. And second, they are inviting to one and all, inducing friends and family to sit back and raise a toast. You know it as soon as you walk in, that something special that just makes you want to move in for a few days or a year. I can't tell you how many times I have walked into a home and instantly felt relaxed. It is as much about the decoration and design as the people who live there.

EXUDING WARMTH

The high cathedral ceilings in this Spanish-style home allow for walls of art and large scale plants, which give the space extra depth and height. This is a living room that screams of warmth and understated elegance. The French doors, on the left side of the room, open up to a lushly covered patio that allows natural light in at all hours of the day. This is great because it limits the need for lamps. The vintage chandelier in the center of the room lends a sense of age and sophistication while not overpowering the serene tone of the room. The saltillo tiles installed throughout the house are not only a wonderful design choice, but also keep the living room cool during the hottest of days. The Persian rug was placed to bring a central focal point to the living room. It also connects with some of the owner's Middle Eastern design influences.

PLAYING WITH COLOR AND TEXTURE

Jesse Acevedo's home is transformed by an exuberant use of color and texture. The mix of contemporary furniture, antiques, and works of art are woven together in an extremely inviting way. The clean lines of the couch and chairs are set against stacks of books and pillows, creating a comfortable and pleasing environment, clean, unfettered, and stylish. Even though the walls are bare, the room is meant to have that slightly unfinished look, a confident stand-on-its-own approach. The beautifully carved wood sculpture of the Madonna that sits on the mantel along with a very large painting that rests against the wall, actually complete the room quite nicely. The blast of vibrant colors is at once fresh and new, but understated at the same time since it doesn't overwhelm nor take away from any other part of the room. This is also a great example of how a room doesn't need a lot of art on the walls.

A LOFTY SETTING

The first thing you might notice when looking at Justus Grimalda's living room is its loftlike qualities. Large scale windows run the length of an entire wall offering a generous amount of natural light. The vast open space also gives the impression that this home is much larger than its 600 square feet.

Being that the living and dining rooms have no defined space, as there would be in a more traditional setup, it was important that all elements flowed easily. Measuring out specific boundary areas is a good way to start, especially to determine how much furniture to use in each area. Comfortable yet stylish furniture was important to Justus since he likes to entertain frequently. He also wanted furniture that was low backed, so as not to block

any views. A great way to make a conventional conversation area is to place an area rug at its center. In this case a large white shag rug was chosen and paired with a round-mirrored contemporary table that is stylish and light reflective. The white lacquered entertainment center hides all the wires and audio visual equipment while the plasma television on the wall functions as a piece of art would.

The dining room table and chairs were given their own area away from the rest of the living space but placed conveniently near the kitchen and countertops. The colors chosen for the walls and art are serene and calming. Earth tones such as browns and greens have a soothing effect and soften the contemporary lines of the space.

A 1950s LOOK

Beth Broderick Paetty is a dedicated cook. She and her husband Scott often entertain. This explains why they were looking for a large space with a big kitchen, a fireplace, and a lot of available light. When they walked into this 4000 square foot 1950s architectural space, they knew they had found their home.

The rooms were all lined with the old fashioned crank windows of the era which lit up the entire space naturally. The closets were huge, which was an added benefit. In addition there were many built-in elements that were specific to the 1950s. The hardware was all gold and the walls and carpets were white. All these great features provided Beth and Scott with a fantastic backdrop.

The first piece purchased for this home was a white Russian Baby Grand piano, which set the tone for the rest of the pieces that would be chosen. The couple had previously bought two large blue sofas that worked great with the rest of their country style furniture in the Craftsman home they had lived in before. These sofas have since been recovered in off-white leatherette and

transformed into 1950s set pieces. The two faux mink recliners scouted by friends, flank the white sofas perfectly. Accents and details such as a period chandelier and a mirror framed in white leather are what make the design in this home complete and cohesive.

Sometimes using a monochromatic color scheme is a difficult undertaking, but in this room it clearly works.

Except for the brown chairs, which add depth to the room, the color palette of white and off-white unifies this large area in a cohesive and friendly manner. In addition to the subtle colors, the wonderful mixture of design sensibilities from the more modern lines of the bar to the more traditional approach of the coffee table further serves to make this a fun and very livable room.

BALANCING ARCHITECTURE AND DESIGN

The architecture of Phil Hammond's condominium building was unmistakably modern. So it was completely inappropriate that his home was full of crown moldings and raised panel doors and cabinetry. The first step was to draw out the finer elements of the home and combine those with some great modern designs. Although it wasn't Phil's intent to fill the house exclusively with authentic mid-century modern pieces, he did mean to select pieces that effortlessly blended with a modern aesthetic. Also important in his selection was the comfort level that the furnishings would provide his guests.

The large surface walls throughout the living spaces were painted in neutral colors. Bold colors were reserved for furnishings and small accessories.

While the living room is of a good size, the space was given the illusion of more room by borrowing the extended site lines that the outdoor space provided. All the existing decorative elements that did not support the original intent of the building's architecture were removed. All moldings, raised panel cabinetry, and trellis work were

trashed. Excessive use of mirrors produced an over-whelming effect, so most of the mirrors were removed as well. However, the smoked mirror over the fireplace was useful in combination with the dark-framed windows and bronze-painted walls to make the back wall "disap-pear" and allow the eye to travel out the windows. The view of the lighted walls and plants beyond brings the outdoors in and makes the space feel larger.

By up lighting the walls beyond the windows, the lighted surfaces define the edges of the space, also func-tioning to bring the outdoors in and enlarge the space.

By replacing the tile patio with a raised wood deck, the floor appears to continue uninterrupted to the out-doors. Orienting the decking in the same direction of the interior flooring reinforces the connection between the indoors and outdoors.

CREATING A CENTER

It was very important for Gregory and Emily to have a real living room in which to spend time together and with their cats. They also like to get together with friends for potlucks, parties, and game nights. This West-facing room has a large window that looks out onto beautiful sunsets that color the neighborhood that they love so much. Whereas the other rooms in the apartment tend to have a cooler palette, this room was purposefully made warmer with yellow walls. The room instantly becomes more welcoming. As such, it now serves as the nerve center of the apartment.

The two reproduction case study daybeds and coffee table from the 1950s are perfect for creating a lighter and more spacious room. The daybeds/sofas are great because they easily convert into sleeping beds for guests. Extra seating is provided by the orange ball chair that looks like a piece of art at first glance. All these elements are clearly practical and space-saving in their design.

The stereo cabinet and components are vintage 1970s. As a decorative touch, Emily displays her collection of printing blocks on the mirror. Terrarium globes are also suspended from the ceiling. This adds flare to the overall look of the room, while bringing the outside in!

LITERARY PASSION
AND FAVORITE COLORS

In renovating Luigi's 1920s Spanish Colonial home, it was important to respect the architectural integrity of the original design, even though it had gone through countless bad restorations over the last eighty years.

The living room is blessed with windows on every side. The natural and bright light allowed for the staining of the floors in a rich dark mahogany. The beams were also painted dark brown, which when juxtaposed with the white ceiling, made them stand out. For Luigi, it was also imperative that the room had a place for books and other objects. Books can give a room a more lived in feeling, which is important since this room is the heart of the house. To accommodate his literary passion, floor-to-ceiling built-in shelves and cabinets were designed to cover the entire length of the wall. These shelves gave the room an added sense of height and depth. The piece was meant to look like it was built when the original structure was built more than eight decades earlier.

A lover of beige and white, Luigi wanted subtle variations of these two colors to envelope the space. The palette of neutral colors keeps the room warm and friendly, allowing for the furniture and accessories to take center stage. With hints of red and cobalt blue added throughout, the living room becomes the perfect place to read a book, enjoy conversations with friends, or simply take a nap.

A WORLDLY LIVING ROOM

Carmen Lopez has seen the world. For every place she has traveled, she has bought something to remind her of the people and culture of that location. Sometimes it was a simple item such as a beautiful shell. Another time she bought an ornate hand painted chandelier. With an eclectic taste and a passion for sophisticated design, this living room is distinguished through contrasting styles of furniture which discerningly compliment one another as well as the space they inhabit. The soft yellow palette chosen for the walls allows everything from the fireplace to the red coral lamp to pop, thus creating a visual harmony that makes you want to find more gems hidden in plain sight.

The use of small accessories, books, and works of art liberally but carefully placed throughout the room, add to the overall luxurious feel. The rich colored drapery hanging down from just below the ceiling gives the room the effect of having high ceilings. Plush and heavily textured fabrics also add opulence to the area.

ONE FINE ROOM

Aiming for a comfortable loftlike feel in this 250 square foot room, there was to be no delineation between dining and living space. The concept for this great room was about functionality and light, not size. Since more than half the wall space in this room is made up of windows, it became a conscious decision to keep all the furniture below the window line so as not to block the natural light from entering the space. This allowed the natural light to bounce off the glass and other reflective surfaces, thus creating the illusion of a bigger area. Opaque and clear glass panels were deliberately used to give the room some privacy from the street, while allowing for natural light to enter.

An avid horticulturalist, it was important to Kevin to bring as much of the outdoors in as possible. He likes to call it "classic California living." I agree that California is the perfect place for living outside-in. Living art in the form of plants, flowers, and old growth bonsai fill every room of this small 525 square foot, one bedroom home. Varying flora add an unexpected palette of vibrant colors and textures to this home and bring a healthier feeling to it as well.

Artwork from around the world has also been seamlessly integrated into the design scheme. Textiles from Bali live peacefully next to sculptures from Africa. Contemporary American and European paintings and some black-and-white and color photographs that he took also adorn the space. These pieces soften the harder edges of the stainless steel window casements and other modern pieces of furniture that can be cold and sterile if not in the proper setting.

INSPIRATION IS EVERYWHERE

The masculine furniture, coordinated color palette, and black-and-white photos of New York City evoke a gentleman's library. The 1913 cottage with original hand-carved moldings and built-in furniture serves as a backdrop for Don's frequent entertaining. Several large scale pieces of furniture are grouped in quiet yet bold seating arrangements that allow for people to get acquainted without feeling overwhelmed.

The combined living and dining room areas create a large open space. These rooms, however, are very distinctive in their own right and have a design directive that was important to Don. Architectural beams painted in a soft white on the living room ceiling convey that you are leaving the room and entering the dining area.

The colors chosen were important to the overall look and feel of the room. Don found the colors in his favorite hotel lobby. Inspiration can be found anywhere and Don found his in a place that made him feel like he was at home. The exact formula of the custom color had to be gently coerced out of the engineers. The paint was liberally applied in several coats that bathed the room in a warm rich glow. When lamps and overhead lighting are used, the color almost fades into the background allowing the furniture and artwork to shine.

CLEAN AND GLAMOROUS

The high arches and generously proportioned windows in Christine Salmon's living room create a warm and inviting living space. The yellows and creams running throughout the room define the warmth. The grouping of larger scale furniture, such as the sofa, with classically tailored lines of a diminutive wing chair and several side tables, reveal a glamorous personality and a light, clean look. This space conveys high country style with a contemporary twist.

The decorative screen at the far end of the room nicely frames the furnishings in front of it, thus creating a stunning vignette while also providing a measure of privacy when the curtains are opened.

The architecturally designed double crown molding conveys a finished look to the room while its placement, so close to the ceiling line, emphasizes the illusion of great height.

A SMALL YET MULTIFUNCTIONAL ROOM

In this small area, seating and entertaining space is limited. It was necessary to create an area that was multifunctional and efficient. The c-shaped side tables are narrow and long, creating a place to set food and drink. They do not impede the walkway or seating areas as they slide into the seat of the couch when necessary.

The two ottomans in front of the couch have dual purposes. First, they can be used for additional seating for guests. Second, they are sturdy enough to act as a table. The couch coverts to a queen-size bed creating another sleeping area.

The color and tone of the artwork compliment the furniture as the palate stays very coordinated. The animals in the jungle painting match the faux zebra-striped ottomans. The painting of a ballerina is done in warm earth tones to keep the organic feel of the living space consistent.

The TV stand creates ample storage for stereo equipment, magazines, and DVDs, thus creating clean surfaces and a place to hide all of the wires. Clutter free and good to look at, this piece of contemporary furniture ties this transitional, but small living area together.

LIVING ROOM TIPS

The living room is usually the most trafficked room in your home. Plan accordingly and place furniture so as not to inhibit walking or entertaining.

Choose a focal point in the room and decorate around it. This will make furniture, art, and plant placement much easier.

Tall plants in corners of your living room will give the room depth and make it look larger. Place a soft spotlight on the floor in front of the plant for a more dramatic effect in the evening.

Don't cram furniture against the wall. Give each piece some breathing room. The living room will look bigger and you won't feel the need to clutter.

Place a small area rug with an interesting design and color scheme over existing carpeting or a larger rug. This will create a whole new look for your room.

Remove accessories and other small collectibles that have been sitting out for a long time. They can make a room look dated. Replace them with other things that you treasure.

CHAPTER 11

Seating Areas

SINCE I LIKE TO ENTERTAIN, I ALWAYS WANT MY HOME TO BE INVITING AND COMFORTABLE. I LOVE WHEN I FIND AN OBVIOUS VOID IN A ROOM WHERE THE ROOM IS NOT BIG ENOUGH TO COMPLETELY DIVIDE INTO TWO AREAS. THIS IS THE PERFECT OPPORTUNITY TO CREATE A SEATING AREA. I AM TALKING ABOUT AN ADDITIONAL "MINI ROOM." AT TIMES IT MAY ONLY INCLUDE ENOUGH ROOM FOR ONE PERSON TO SIT, BUT OFTEN IT IS AN INVITING SCENE FOR A ROMANTIC COUPLE OR A SMALL GROUP OF FRIENDS.

I CREATE THESE SPACES USING SOFAS, CHAIRS, BENCHES, OR EVEN PILLOWS LAID OUT ON THE FLOOR. YOU CAN CREATE ANY ENVIRONMENT BY ADDING COLOR, PLANTS AND FLOWERS, AND BOOKS AND CANDLES. JUST REMEMBER, YOU DON'T HAVE TO BUY LARGE PIECES OF FURNITURE JUST SO MORE PEOPLE CAN SIT. FIGURE OUT WHAT WILL WORK AND HOW MUCH YOU ULTIMATELY NEED AND WANT.

A PLACE FOR QUIET CONVERSATION

Mary Randleman's formative years spent in Cuba have left a lasting impression on her design aesthetic. She believes in classic and comfortable living that combines a dose of humor and a pop of color.

This vignette is part of a larger living room that is surrounded by walls of windows and French doors. However, she considered this particular corner dead space. It is an area just feet from the front foyer and needed to be warmed up. Now guests enter into the home in a more intimate and comforting environment.

Knowing that this could be made into a backdrop for quiet conversation, a high-backed and delicately carved painted screen made out of wood Indian doors was placed behind a beautiful Louis XV settee with a carved walnut frame. Indian block patterned fabric in a lustrous blue-and-white pattern is completed with a generous down cushion and a slightly oversize pillow.

Ultimately, decorative dividers soften what could be a jarring transition from one room to another. They create a level of anticipation as to what is on the other side.

VINTAGE SEATING

These wonderful 1930s era chairs were in terrible condition when picked up at a garage sale. The fabric was threadbare while the springs were coming out on all sides rendering the chair unusable.

New velvet fabric and gentle refinishing brought back the natural beauty of these chairs. Piping added to the fabric gives depth and a look that might have been the original designer's intent. The red phone on the table has a great vintage appeal and picks up the fall colors of the painting hanging above.

BATHROOM ALTERNATIVE

This is a great way to increase the seating area in your bathroom and also warm up a room should it be a bit cold. This bathtub, while in great shape was not utilized as often as the shower, creating wasted space that could otherwise be used. A thick piece of wood was covered in white fabric and placed over the tub. A cushion was custom sized to fit on top of the wood and several pillows were added to create a very inviting day bed. Should you move out, the tub is still there and in pristine condition.

BEDROOM CORNER

This corner of the master bedroom is turned into a luxurious setting that will never bore you. The traditional oversize armchair with a firm yet extraordinarily comfortable cushion and matching ottoman is just what you want after a long day of work. An accent pillow matches the wall color, which is a nice touch, while the curtains add a bit of pizzazz and flavor. The cashmere throw and some favorite magazines truly make this a relaxing and peaceful place to read.

THE RUG AND COFFEE TABLE SPICE THINGS UP

In this setting, the faux leopard skin rug adds flair to the neutral colored sisal rug underneath. Its spotted pattern doesn't conflict with the color on the walls since there is no busy wallpaper or designs to contend with. The shape also makes for a different look than a square or round one would, creating interest in the space. If there had been busy wall coverings, a patterned area rug would not have worked in this spot. Placing an interesting area rug is also a way to accent your room without worrying about additional accessories or artwork. The glass coffee table is a nice way to open up the area creating a light and spacious feel.

Make sure the rug under the coffee table is large enough for all four legs to fit comfortably.

A NOOK BECOMES A SEAT

Many times, a room will have that one space that you just don't know what to do with, creating an interior design headache. In this bedroom a small nook was formed when a closet was taken out to widen the entry. Because it is only about twenty inches deep, not many things fit without it feeling crowded. I like to make a room as functional as possible. A console wasn't an option since it would have fought with a grouping of shelves I had already placed across from it. Eventually, a custom-size bench covered in a black cowhide with a select group of colorful pillows was placed, creating an inviting area to sit and relax. The twentieth-century decoupage painting was hung above the bench to give a sophisticated and somewhat whimsical flare.

These particular pillows were chosen because their colors are coordinated with the colors of the painting and dress up the white walls with some pop and sizzle.

SEATING AREA TIPS

A seating area can be one chair and a table, a few pillows on the floor, or several pieces of furniture arranged with a design in mind. Create a space that fits your lifestyle and how you use your home.

Have various lighting options at your disposal. If overhead lighting is too bright or doesn't convey the right mood you want to set, then floor and table lamps, or even candles, may be in order.

If you have a large room, creating several seating areas is a great way to make a space feel more intimate.

Place objects in the seating area that make you smile when you see them.

Make the area visually stimulating with a jolt of color and interesting accessories.

Have the flexibility to create additional seating areas should you need to. There is nothing wrong with designing out of the box; it's sometimes half the fun.

CHAPTER 12

Indoor/
Outdoor

WHETHER ON THE WEST COAST, EAST COAST, NORTH, OR SOUTH, EVERYONE LOVES SPENDING TIME OUTDOORS WHEN THE WEATHER IS NICE. I BELIEVE THAT MERGING THE INDOORS AND OUTDOORS IS NOT ONLY WONDERFUL DESIGN, BUT IS ALSO A VERY HEALTHY WAY TO LIVE ONE'S LIFE. THE EASIEST WAY TO BRING THE OUTSIDE IN IS BY USING PLANTS. I'M LUCKY TO BE SPENDING MOST OF MY TIME ON THE WEST COAST WHERE INDOOR/OUTDOOR LIVING IS EASY AND EXPECTED. BUT NO MATTER WHERE YOU LIVE, TAKE ADVANTAGE OF NATURE'S NATURAL BEAUTY, EVEN IF IT'S ONLY FOR A FEW MONTHS A YEAR!

INSIDE OUT AND OUTSIDE IN

At Phil Hammond's house, bamboo fencing and outdoor icicle lights on one patio wall are an important aspect of this outdoor seating area. In the day, the lights disappear, but at night the back-lit bamboo makes an inviting atmosphere that draws people out of the living room. Built-in seating at the perimeter of the deck takes full advantage of the small patio by placing the seating at the exterior limits. The flush pool of water is tucked under a low table, saving space while combining the two elements for a more dramatic focal point from indoors. Red tiles and lighting in the pool add yet more visual impact.

Vines that are growing on the neighbor's building are utilized by up-lighting them so they are seen from the indoors at night creating a stunning backdrop. Very simple plantings keep the tiny space from feeling cluttered.

Originally, the area in this photo was entirely enclosed, choking off light from the den and a number of other rooms. The ceiling was removed and replaced with a pergola during the renovation. Also, new waterproof tile and a drainage system were introduced to assist in maintenance while the black wrought iron furniture was painted white to give a more aged look. The yellow outdoor fabric on the cushions keep everything looking light and airy all year. This room has since become a great place to gather for a glass of wine before dinner and functions as the "smoking room" during parties. The candles add a wonderful aroma to the evening sky and create areas for intimate conversation.

BIG WINDOWS

This beautiful contemporary condominium with sweeping city views called for a living area that would open up to the deck. The use of floor-to-ceiling glass doors allow for the indoor/outdoor feeling to exist even when the sliding doors are closed. The lush plantings, inside and out, creates a cohesive transition and unites the interior and the exterior seamlessly. The contemporary outdoor sitting area is carefully centered on the window, making the entire space work as one.

Indoor/outdoor living was an essential element in Christine Salmon's design plan. She wanted a space where indoor and out unite in a central courtyard. The outdoor entertainment and dining area connects directly to the kitchen and two bedrooms, creating a nucleus for the home and ultimately the impression of a much larger space.

Because Christine has been living in the house for a while, she knew the space well and made notes as to the sun's patterns and windier spots versus calmer areas. Ultimately, Christine decided on a large fireplace as the backyard focal point.

Additional seating and counter space was created by building a long shelf that extended from both sides of the fireplace. The plain concrete flooring was jazzed up with several coats of a rustic brown paint. The color not only complemented the fireplace but also the colors of the floors in Christine's home, which served to unite the disparate areas. She also bridged the inside and out by liberally using potted plants and accessories on the inside. A tall trellis with large wood beams was installed and an Italian country dining table added. Sheer curtains were hung to give a sense of privacy and to create a room-like effect.

This room blends mid-century aesthetics with Moroccan overtones. It is a great example of someone who truly lives an indoor/outdoor lifestyle. Concrete floors and Lucite furniture give way to an outdoor space filled with overstuffed cushions, candles, and a glorious daybed. The direct sun is kept at bay by two white fabric panels creating a tented and nomadic feeling.

INDOOR/OUTDOOR TIPS

Bring various potted plants inside your home over the course of the year.

Plan your indoor and outdoor design simultaneously. This will allow for cohesiveness in the overall design of your home.

Floor-to-ceiling sliding glass doors are the best idea for smooth transitions.

Similar plants that border doorways on both sides, both indoors and outdoors, help create an illusion that the two spaces are actually one in the same.

Water features create an environment of sound that brings both areas together.

Translucent, transparent, or no window coverings allow for natural light to enter a room at all times.

RESOURCES

Home Furnishings and Accessories
Mogul
8262 Melrose Avenue
Los Angeles, CA 90046
323.658. 5130
Contemporary furniture, original art,
Classic vintage mid-century furnishings

Waterford
www.waterford.com
1-800-955-1550
Waterford Wedgwood is the world's largest
luxury lifestyle crystal and ceramics company.
In addition to Waterford Crystal, Waterford
Wedgwood includes the premium lifestyle
brands: Wedgwood, Rosenthal, and Royal Doulton

Interior Designers
XOL: Design
8671 Wilshire Blvd., Suite 400
Beverly Hills, CA 90211
310.601.3203
www.xoldesign.com

Randelman Residence
Mary Randelman Interior Decoration
6531 W. 6th Street
Los Angeles, CA 90049
310.295.7875
www.woodtilly@aol.com

Hammond Residence
Cole Garrison
337 North Oakhurst Drive
Beverly Hills, CA 90210
310.614.2011
dcgarrison@hotmail.com

CREDITS

Written by: **Eduardo Xol**

Cowritten by: **Steve Miller**

Contributing Writers: **Monica Cajayon and Leah Matuson**

Edited by: **Monica Cajayon for XOL: Creative**

Photography by: **Doug Myers**

Photography Assistant: **Clarissa Shull**

Cover Makeup: **Michelle Spieler**

Additional Makeup: **Tracy Anderson**

Art Direction: **Steve Miller and Eduardo Xol**
for XOL: Creative

Design Assistant: **Desiree Neil for XOL: Design**

Chapter 1

Page 3: Ho-Han living room; page 4: BroderickPaetty lamp; page 5: Acevedo living room; page 6: Lopez dining room and Acevedo bedroom.

Chapter 2

Pages 8–9: Acevedo bedroom; page 11: Grimalda bedroom; pages 12–13: Acevedo bedroom; pages 14–15: Acevedo guest bedroom; pages 16–17: Broderick Paetty bedroom; pages 18–19: Grimalda residence; pages 20–21: Hammond bedroom; page 22: Ho-Han bedroom; page 23: Loerke bedroom; page 24: Morris bedroom; page 25: Randelman bedroom; pages 26–27: Randelman guest bedroom.

Chapter 3

Pages 28–29: Acevedo bedroom; page 30: Ho-Han residence; page 31: Randelman living room, Broderick Paetty residence, Lopez residence; page 32: Acevedo bathroom, Ho-Han kitchen; page 33: Irauzqui kitchen, Acevedo kitchen; page 35: Miller/Navarro bedroom; page 36: Irauzqui living room; page 37: Randelman living room, Lopez bedroom, Irauzqui living room; page 38: Randelman living room; page 39: Randelman master bedroom; page 40: Ho-Han bathroom; page 41: Lopez bathroom; page 42: Lopez breakfast nook; page 43: Lopez dining room; pages 44–45: Kadel/Namias kitchen; page 47: Acevedo residence, Morris residence; pages 48–49: Randelman closet.

Chapter 4

Pages 50–51: Hammond bathroom; page 53: Broderick Paetty bathroom; page 54: Hammond powder room; page 55: Broderick Paetty guest bathroom; pages 56–57: Grimalda master bathroom; pages 58–59: Drewry master bathroom; page 60: Hammond bathroom; page 61: Morris bathroom; pages 62–63: Loerke master bathroom; pages 64–65: Lopez guest bathroom; pages 66–67: Miller/Navarro cabana bathroom; pages 68–69: Miller/Navarro guest bathroom; pages 70–71: Miller/Navarro master bathroom; page 73: Randelman bathroom, Salmon bathroom; pages 74–75: Winston bathroom; pages 76–77: Acevedo master bathroom; pages 78–79: Acevedo guest bathroom.

Chapter 5

Pages 80–81: Salmon residence; page 82: Acevedo residence; page 83: (upper left) bedroom fixture, Broderick Paetty residence, Acevedo residence, Randelman residence; page 84: Broderick Paetty residence, Broderick Paetty residence, Randelman residence; page 85: Acevedo residence, Hammond residence; page 86: Lopez residence, Broderick Paetty residence; page 87: Hammond residence, Morris residence; page 88: Acevedo residence, Lopez residence; page 89: Acevedo residence.

ACKNOWLEDGMENTS

First and foremost, I would like to thank Steve Miller, my coauthor and creative partner. Without his tireless support, faith, and talent, this book would have never happened. Our hard work is paying off my friend! I'd also like to thank his partner Steve Navarro for his patience and understanding of the long hours it has taken to make *Home Sense* happen.

I'd like to thank my family including Eduardo Sr., my dad; Mirna, my mom; Ernesto, my brother; and especially Monica, my sister, for her support and participation as a contributor in this book. Also a big thanks to my extended family. *¡Por su apoyo y la fe de nuestra Mamá Catita estoy viviendo mis sueños!*

Gracias to my team at XOL: Design and XOL: Creative, Stephen, Desiree, and Brittany. To Arlette at Revolution Design. To my agent, Carlos Carreras, and everyone else at UTA. To my attorney and great friend, David Colden, and his staff at Colden, McKuin and Frankel. To Andy Cohen and the team at Magna Global, and my new team at PMK/HBH, Britt and Annie . . . let's make some noise!

A big gracious hug to my family at *Extreme Makeover: Home Edition* for putting up with me on my computer in our trailer, Ty, Michael, Tanya, Ed, Paige, Paul, Preston, Tracy, and Johnny. To my EPs, Denise Cramsey and Tim Warren, and a special thanks to Tom Forman for giving me the opportunity to work and design interiors on our wonderful show. To the rest of production who have filled my life with joy and to the families that have given me the opportunity to make a difference. You have changed my life forever!

To those of you that have been my angels, I will be eternally grateful for your faith in, and support of, me. Richard Perez-Feria for teaching me to "own it," to Julie Link, Karen Gruber, Tanya Nierhoff, Danny Salas, Christopher Grubb, and all who pushed for me from the beginning of this phase in my career!

To everyone at Endemol, especially David Goldberg, Rob Smith, and Lisa Higgins; everyone at ABC especially Steve McPhereson, Andrea Wong, Vicky Dummer, and Amy Entelis; and the crew over at *ABC News* and *Good Morning America*, Charles Gibson, Diane Sawyer, Robin Roberts, Mike Barz, Luz Montez, and Anthony Underwood for their support on my segments.

To my *gente* at *People en Español*, for your support over the last year and in my "Casa" column! Especially Jackie, Carmen, Lourdes, and Erika: *¡Las quiero mucho!*

Of course . . . to my good friends, Fabian, Richard, and JL: your unconditional love drives me to be a better person! A special thanks to Elliot Potts . . . you know why!

To anyone else I may have forgotten, and you know who you are, know that as I sit here in the middle of a cornfield in North Dakota, that I am sending out vibrations of gratitude and blessings to all of you.

GO FORTH AND HAVE FUN!
I CAN'T WAIT TO SEE WHAT YOU
COME UP WITH!

~Eduardo Xol